C000131020

'I wish I'd had the benefit of this book 40 years ago—its wisdom would have significantly shortened my own fraught journey towards truly understanding what effective leadership was all about, especially at the one level that in my opinion really counts in the armed forces, junior combat leadership. Connolly in *The Commando Way* lucidly and self-effacingly draws upon his own rapid and often cathartic journey up through the ranks to acquire this wisdom through first-hand and often grim experience. With broad military combat exposure . . . Connolly can indeed speak with authority on the subject of leadership at the coal face. I believe this book should be essential reading for all aspiring leaders including at both officer and NCO's schools, which reflects the universality of its relevance.' — *General Mike Hindmarsh AO, DSC, CSC, former commander of the Australian Forces in the Middle East*

'*The Commando Way* is a gritty, honest and inciteful memoir that describes an incredible journey from the unique perspective of a Special Forces operative. It is so much more than a military memoir. It is the story of growth—the growth of a soldier, a leader, a man and a human. Bram Connolly shares the invaluable lessons he has learnt in his extraordinary life about leadership, resilience, teamwork and human performance, all from the lens of a person who authentically believes that one's values underpins everything we say, do and model for those around us. That's why I was gripped by this book and admire the author greatly. A must read for all leaders, change makers and innovators.' — *Rabia Siddique, international humanitarian, speaker, author*

'You're so immersed in the true story telling of this book that you forget how much you are learning along the way.' — *Merrick Watts*

'Bram Connolly's latest book *The Commando Way* is a gritty review of his life in the military during an exceptional period of modern history. His raw description of his military experiences and the hard lessons he has learnt can be applied to people currently serving in the military and to those trying to find their way in corporate life . . . I would highly recommend *The Commando Way* to aspiring leaders of all ages. The lessons at the end of each chapter are gold dust . . .'
— *Brigadier Mark Smethurst (Ret'd) DSC, AM, former deputy commander Special Operations Command*

'Bram's approach has always been no-nonsense, functional and highly effective, and his method has been perfectly distilled in *The Commando Way*. This book is a great balance of all things leadership, self-improvement and human optimisation, and will be an effective tool for everyday people right through to elite performers in the sporting, military and business worlds.' — *Ian Prior, captain Western Force rugby team*

'The scientific research shows that leadership is both discovered as well as developed. We oftentimes discover it in the least expected moments and develop it with the right practice during the mundane moments. Bram's book brilliantly outlines the blueprint for both. This is not only a thrilling read but also a deep leadership manual.' — *Patrycja Slawuta, MA, PhD(c) Psych, psychologist, researcher and mindhacker*

Calling in Air Support, Afghanistan, October 2010

THE
COMMANDO
WAY

Other books by Bram Connolly

The Fighting Season
Off Reservation

BRAM CONNOLLY THE COMMANDO WAY

A SPECIAL FORCES COMMANDER'S LESSONS FOR LIFE, LEADERSHIP AND SUCCESS

ALLEN&UNWIN
SYDNEY·MELBOURNE·AUCKLAND·LONDON

All unsourced quotes at the start of chapters are the author's.

First published in 2020

Copyright © Bram Connolly 2020

All rights reserved. No part of this book may be reproduced or transmitted in any form or by any means, electronic or mechanical, including photocopying, recording or by any information storage and retrieval system, without prior permission in writing from the publisher. The Australian *Copyright Act 1968* (the Act) allows a maximum of one chapter or 10 per cent of this book, whichever is the greater, to be photocopied by any educational institution for its educational purposes provided that the educational institution (or body that administers it) has given a remuneration notice to the Copyright Agency (Australia) under the Act.

Allen & Unwin
83 Alexander Street
Crows Nest NSW 2065
Australia
Phone: (61 2) 8425 0100
Email: info@allenandunwin.com
Web: www.allenandunwin.com

 A catalogue record for this book is available from the National Library of Australia

ISBN 978 1 76052 863 8

Set in 12/17 pt Minion Pro by Midland Typesetters, Australia
Printed and bound in Australia by Griffin Press, part of Ovato

10 9 8 7 6 5 4 3 2 1

 The paper in this book is FSC® certified. FSC® promotes environmentally responsible, socially beneficial and economically viable management of the world's forests.

In memory
Colonel Johannes Cornelis Fleer AM, DCM (1949–2013)

Like many others, I am in your debt.
You showed us what good leadership looks like.

CONTENTS

A NOTE FROM PAUL ROOS

Having read many books on personal development, leadership and culture, it was refreshing to read Bram's amazing story with actionable solutions. His ability to take literal life and death situations and normalise them is exceptional.

Most of us will never know what it is like to put your life on the line. The stories of survival he tells are extreme and you can't help but be inspired by incredible acts of bravery.

For Bram to share these stories is a gift in itself. But he doesn't make you feel inadequate or guilty.

He takes the stories and his training and articulates them into insightful lessons. These lessons then provide a great road map for success. After reading the book I often found myself reflecting on them.

Transitioning from sport to the corporate world I regularly pass on my experiences and I will highly recommend this book as another tool to great leadership.

I have always asked, 'Do you want to be part of the problem or the solution?' This book is definitely part of the solution.

A NOTE FROM GENERAL STANLEY McCHYRSTAL (RET'D)

Leadership has been studied in one way or another for millennia. The fundamental debate still rages—is leadership an art, a science, or both?

There are some who believe, for good reason, that leadership is a clear set of characteristics—a pure science. This theory contends leaders are those who are born with and can apply a certain blend of attributes. This theory, while easier to understand, betrays the nuance of context. It does not acknowledge the reality in which we live—a reality that requires understanding leadership as a relationship between the leader, the follower and the context.

There is no doubt that certain characteristics and behaviours lend themselves to effective leadership better than others. Some are born with the characteristics and self-discipline of a leader and are able to naturally inspire a team. Conversely, people can learn and develop the knowledge, skills, and attitude required to motivate and provide direction—to assist others in pursuing a shared vision. There is both an art and a science to leadership.

Bram Connolly himself is perfectly placed to write about this subject. He has lived it from the moment he joined the army as a 17-year-old until well after he departed fulltime service. He is an authentic leader who shares his journey, so that others might become better leaders themselves. Bram's experiences range from being a new recruit, to a young 19-year-old soldier deployed to Somalia and then to the head of Selection Wing for the Australian Special Forces. He learnt lessons from the dark jungles of Far North Queensland to the open *dascht* of Afghanistan—and he shares these candid experiences with you so that you can see what he saw, feel what he felt, and understand what he learnt from these profound moments.

The learnings from Bram's book will help you to put in place authentic strategies to improve your own life, develop your own leadership style, and help others on their journey too.

I'm sure this book will become required reading for junior military officers and soldiers, emergency services and first responders, and anyone else who has any desire to be better at the elusive skill of leadership.

Former commander of US and International Security Assistance Forces Afghanistan and former commander of the United States' Joint Special Operations Command

AUTHOR'S NOTE

'To be a good leader you have to first be a good
follower, but to be a great leader you have to
remember that being a good follower wasn't easy.'

It was no accident that the first couple of books I wrote were military fiction. I made it known to my publisher, the wonderful Rebecca Kaiser from Allen & Unwin, that I didn't want to write yet another ex-Special Forces operator's first-hand account of his military career. Practically every member of the Australian Special Forces community—and the wider Australian Defence Force, for that matter—has a great story to tell. At least, that certainly seems to be the case at around 10 am on Anzac Day. I'm not so narcissistic to think that my life, or my career, have been so noteworthy that they would capture the reading public's hearts and minds more than those of any other operator.

Over the years, though, I've had many conversations with Rebecca about my career. We first met when I agreed to check some of the acronyms and military terms in Chris Masters' book *Uncommon Soldier*. We talked a lot about his experiences working with the Special Operations Task Group in Afghanistan. Later, our conversations would turn to the projects I was working on, including my mentoring and leadership consultancy, Hindsight Leadership and Resilience, and my podcast, *The WarriorU Podcast*. Our conversations invariably led back to me writing a non-fiction account of my military career.

I was cautious about the prospect. My mindset has always been that I'm an average guy, and that it's because I'm average that I've been lucky to have the career I've had. I believed that the average person had to work harder and strive more than those with a genetic predisposition to greatness. But I also felt that average people couldn't risk wasting an opportunity. With this in mind, I eventually agreed to write an account of my experiences. Perhaps I could help other people realise that they too can achieve great things, I thought, if they could just admit to being average. Indeed, the book's working title was *The Risk of Being Average*—my belief was that if I named the book in this way, it would allow me to share my experiences in a way I was comfortable with.

When the first draft was finished, I looked it over—and saw that it was complete rubbish. Frankly, the title didn't make any sense. Average people don't get into the Special Forces. Average people don't get awarded Distinguished Service Medals for Leadership. Average people don't serve for five years on the National Counter Terrorism Team, nor do they move up through the ranks from private to major. An average guy who had not attended the Royal Military College just wouldn't be recognised as a student of merit on a professional officer career course either. I was trying to convince myself that I was just an average person, but at the same time convince readers that the things I had done were easily achievable.

The book was rubbish for other reasons too, not the least of which was that I couldn't even answer the simple question: *What is average?* Or, for that matter: *The average of what, exactly?* In the end, the book had me asking a lot more questions of myself than I'd answered for the reader. I acknowledged that I needed to reframe it.

For starters, the book needed a new title, and the content would have to speak to that title throughout. I thought about this deeply, staying up at night and flicking through my manuscript as I tried to work out what it was I'd written. This wasn't writer's block—it was much worse. I was trying to understand who I had been when I was in the Australian Army. For nearly a year, it seemed the book would never see the light of day.

That all changed while I was going for a long run along the coast between Fremantle and Cottesloe, Western Australia, in early 2019. Perhaps it was a mixture of the hot headwind and the onset of mild dehydration, but I had to admit to myself, after all these years, that I wasn't average (whatever it was measured against). If I could admit that, then perhaps I could move forward with my book. I drew from this a new confidence, one I hadn't felt for years since leaving the Army. The book I'd written was a series of hard-fought lessons, I recognised, and some of them were crazy. More than that, though, I saw that the book was a road map of my personal leadership journey.

This book explores my experiences as a soldier. It starts with my time as a private soldier and forward scout in Somalia in 1993. I became a commando team commander in the 4th Battalion of the Royal Australian Regiment (4RAR), now the 2nd Commando Regiment (2CDO) after the first regular Commando Selection Course in 1997. I served as a reconnaissance team commander in East Timor in 2001. I commanded a sniper team in the first National Counter Terrorist Team (Tactical Assault Group – East) in 2003, and then I became a platoon commander in Afghanistan in 2010. I'd held all the junior non-commissioned officer leadership positions, as well as being a platoon sergeant, and my career culminated in my becoming a Special Forces 'Alpha'—the callsign designation for a platoon commander in the 2nd Commando Regiment.

Getting to this point had taken years of dedication and application. I'd learnt much about leadership, teamwork and resilience, and been handed plenty of life lessons along the way, both through my direct experiences and from having incredible mentors. I realised, on that run between Fremantle and Cottesloe, that I had to share all these lessons too.

As far as I was concerned, it was settled: the book would be called *The Commando Way*.

AFGHANISTAN, 2010

Gumbad Valley. I was lying on my back, drenched in sweat, shaking with fear and suppressing the need to piss myself, yet again.

The bullets ripped through the air, slamming into the hard-packed mud walls. Dust and grit showered down on me, settling on my face and in my upturned collar. My neck was already itchy, the dust from the debris mixing with my sweat and camouflage cream.

'Fuck this shit! Seriously, man, just fuck this shit!' I yelled to everyone and nobody. I winced as yet more rounds slammed into the compound behind me. The small clay and straw fence I was lying behind had so far done a good job of preventing the Taliban fighters from killing me and my signaller. *If I could only get my hands on the little prick at the other end of that machine gun fire*, I thought, *I'd tear him apart.*

I was furious at having been ambushed like this. It was as if they had waited until the exact moment I left the protection of the compound to start firing. Of course, they had—that was the whole damn point of an ambush. They'd been chasing my platoon for a few days now, watching us, and waiting—and then BOOM!

I didn't dare lift my head too high for fear of having it blown off. I'd grown to like my head over the years, and thought I'd be better off keeping it for a few more at least. I assumed the fire was coming from a PKM machine gun, a Russian-made weapon renowned for its accuracy, its devastating rate of fire and its ability to function even in the harshest conditions—conditions just like these. They were everywhere in Afghanistan in 2010, and they always seemed to be firing at me.

I glanced at my own rifle: the end of it was full of dirt from when I'd slammed it into the deck while seeking cover behind this low wall. The enemy fire was coming in bursts, and possibly from multiple locations. I couldn't hear the thumps from the points of origin, just the cracks as the rounds zipped past. Angry hornets buzzed above me, over the roof, around the corners—seemingly everywhere. I could hear Taliban voices every now and again too.

The bullets were slamming in at around one each second just above my cowering head. Sometimes they grazed the top of the small wall a few centimetres above my face—the very definition of suppressing fire. I took a deep breath and calmed myself. Lying helpless on my back, and with my impotent rifle beside me, I looked up at the clear blue sky. Every now and then another series of bullets would hit the low wall instead of the compound, and the impact would reverberate through my helmet. The enemy was telling me that my presence was known, and that for the moment he had my measure. This was man on man.

A mountain range dominated the building we had taken refuge in. To the north and east the ground rose up into sharp rocky outcrops that spied over our position. To the south and west another mountain range further out intersected the plateau. In effect we were located on a small pimple, smack bang in the middle of enemy heartland. The compound we were in overlooked smaller buildings running further down the valley and there was a complex mess of creek lines all coming together in the Green Belt providing excellent covered access to any enemy brave enough to want to close in on us. Given all of the rocky peaks and hidden re-entrants climbing up into the mountains, there was no way to know for sure where the Taliban were firing from. If they climbed any higher up into the foothills, though, it was certain that this 'grazing fire'—so named because it travels just a metre or two above the ground—would become 'plunging fire', which dives on you from above. Then we would be proper fucked.

Under normal circumstances in a traditional military setting, grazing fire is considered the ideal way to employ a machine gun. In the Australian military, soldiers are taught the Theory of Machine Gun Fire. The idea is to situate your machine gun so that its fire moves above the ground no more than the height of a standing man. When a round hits its target, this is called the 'first catch', and when it eventually hits the ground after going through its target, this is called the 'first graze'. The distance between these two locations decreases as the distance of the first catch gets further from the weapon that fired it. Why does this matter? Well, ideally the round hits another target after the first one, and so does twice the damage. Two for the price of one, so to speak. So the closer you are to the target, the better your chance of hitting more than one target.

Plunging fire, on the other hand, is generally less desirable, as it is the product of a poorly sited machine gun trying to hit a target that is beyond the range of the weapon. That is, of course, unless you are trying to hit a target that is behind cover or in a low point in the ground. In that case plunging fire is very handy, and that was the situation I found myself in. This plunging fire, normally useless, threatened to bring me and my platoon undone.

The problem with fighting an unconventional enemy is they do things in a military setting you don't expect, because they're not trained to behave like soldiers normally do. In a similar way, boxers and MMA fighters experience this exact same behaviour when sparring with 'inexperienced' opponents. They do unorthodox things, throw punches and kicks from unconventional angles, making them a totally different prospect to most trained and conditioned athletes. Even if your ability far outweighs theirs, it can be surprising when these unskilled, inexperienced fighters clip you.

In war, of course, getting clipped can have completely different consequences. The Taliban probably had no concept about the Theory of Machine Gun Fire, and if you tried to explain it to them, they'd probably laugh in your face and continue lobbing their rounds high in the air, hoping to hit you. Such tactics can be simple yet effective.

Pinned down at the compound in the Gumbad Valley, there was nothing we could do. There was no prospect of air support: we simply had to fight our way out.

My citation for the Distinguished Service Medal (DSM) referred to me darting between positions, gallantly directing fire on enemy locations and changing the tide of the battle—at least, that's the impression you get. The reality was that I was cowering behind a small clay wall getting my arse spanked.

A few minutes earlier, I had left the safety of the fortified building to go and check on the sentry who was watching the creek line to the north—an obvious enemy approach route. The large compound had been used the night before by the other platoon in my company. We had conducted a relief in place in the early hours of the morning. The plan was for them to head further west, securing the route to the extraction point, which we would try to reach by nightfall.

We had been trapped in this valley a week, even though our mission was only meant to last 72 hours. A dust storm in the middle of Afghanistan. If you've been deployed from the safety of a Forward Operating Base, what's known as being 'outside the wire', you'd know how important those assets are. The problem with this protocol was that the Taliban tended to not get the memo.

As a result of this apparent lack of communications between the Regional Command South (RC-S) headquarters and the Taliban's senior leadership, we had been chased down Gumbad Valley in rolling gun battles for three days. Initially I had tried to be aggressive and conduct early-morning fighting patrols, to keep the enemy off-balance and away from our extraction route, but generally they'd slept in and then attacked us in the heat of the day while we rested. We were yet to acclimatise, having been in country less than a few weeks, so our response to their assaults was lacklustre in the 50-degree heat.

Two days ago we ran out of food, and the water finished yesterday. It was very likely we'd be out of ammunition tomorrow. I'd ordered our radios to be switched off the evening before, as most were showing the last red bar of power and we had no fresh batteries. That's why I was now running between teams to pass on messages and get them to turn their radios back on. It was old-school soldiering—only now I seemed to be doing more lying in the dirt than running.

The compound we were holed up in had been used before, but we weren't to know that at this time. It had once been a Dutch outpost, and before that a Russian fort. It was well known to the Taliban and the mujahedin before them, and probably to the British another hundred years before that. The enemy and their foreign fighters were using their local knowledge to great effect.

The radio traffic from the teams was now frantic. All positions were pinned down. The fire coming from the mountain range was incredible. It was like being at the other end of a range shoot at 3 pm on a Friday afternoon, when the company sergeant major has just told the men that he doesn't want any ammunition to come back to base. 'Expend all ammo!' I could hear him yell, and a hundred men did their best to comply.

I took off my helmet, thinking I might just be able to get an eye up above the wall to have a look around. It sounds foolish, but it's not the stupidest thing I've ever done. I lifted myself slowly and peeked around, just exposing the side of my face and head, fully expecting a bullet to the brain. Fortunately, at that exact time the Taliban firing at my position was conducting a reload.

You stupid prick, I grinned to myself. *Gotcha!*

My tormentor wasn't using a PKM machine gun after all, I realised, but its older brother, the AK-47. First designed by Mikhail Kalashnikov not long after World War Two, its basic design has stood the test of time: even today it meets the demands of many armies and fighting groups. In the hands of a skilled adversary, it can make your life quite uncomfortable.

Well, this skilled adversary wasn't up in the mountains, as I'd suspected; he was virtually on our doorstep, lying in the rocks less than a hundred metres from the edge of the ravine. His mates were moving around in there too. We'd been firing up into the hills, way over their heads, and they'd been slowly creeping forward through the complex rock structures that jutted out of the deep creek lines. We were in trouble.

I rolled back and lay flat; I didn't have enough time to get a shot off as he'd already resumed firing at my position. I looked across at my signaller and told him we were about to move. That's when I noticed his 12-foot radio antenna still poking up in the air. 'Jesus Christ, Barns, put it down,' I shouted, gesturing at the offending item, as I adjusted my body armour. More rounds slammed into the wall. 'Yeah and fuck you!' I screamed back at them, kicking my feet up and down like a petulant child. Somewhere up on the roof of the compound, one of my soldiers laughed, finding the sight of his boss pinned down out in the open a right craic.

'Shit, sorry, boss,' said Barns. He lowered the antenna and folded it up, rolling a rubber band off his wrist and wrapping it around the indelible pointer.

I removed a grenade from its pouch on my body armour. Initially, I'd thought about using coloured smoke to cover us, but decided on High Explosive (HE) instead. The Taliban fighter was out of range, but it would make me feel better—and maybe the blast would make one of them poke their heads out and I'd blow it off.

I waited until Barns was ready and then threw the grenade out over the wall. It went about 6 metres and made an almighty bang. I jumped up to my knees and followed it with half a magazine of double-taps, firing through the dust at the enemy's known position, and then at positions in close proximity that looked likely.

As Barns ran to the edge of the next building, I followed behind him, expecting him to cover me. I had a plan, now that the lads had their radios back on. We would only fire back at the enemy with the occasional double-taps, until we were all ready. Then, with communication checks complete, I would give a rolling call over the radio and we would unleash punishment on them—just like we'd been receiving.

I had several different weapons in the platoon to fight back with. Most of my guys were equipped with an M4A-1 assault rifle, whose unique capabilities made it our weapon of choice. It could be fitted with a suppressor, making it harder for our enemy to locate us. It also reduces noise and overpressure in confined environments, making the shooter more combat-effective. Its handiest characteristic was that it had a Rail Adaptor System (RAS), or Picatinny Rail, which allowed a host of accessories to be attached to it. These included sighting systems and laser pointers, as well as the M203 40-millimetre grenade launcher and a variety of shotguns for shooting off door locks and hinges when you really needed to get into a bad guy's house. It was pretty much like Lego for soldiers!

Each six-man team, of which there were four, had a 7.62-millimetre Mk 48 machine gun, which was basically a beefed-up version of the 5.56-millimetre Minimi machine gun. Every second or third man carried an M72A6 66-millimetre rocket launcher, which was extremely useful against fortified structures, to create secondary fragmentation against the enemy, or to create a shock action—as I was about to do.

The last weapon I planned to use to get out of my current pickle was the 84-millimetre Carl Gustaf Medium Direct Fire Support Weapon (MDFSW). Fortunately, I had two in the platoon on this task. My goal was to create a serious headache for the enemy.

I planned to get all my riflemen to fire two magazines per man. That would leave us around a magazine and a half for what might follow. Machine guns (100 rounds), one 66-millimetre rocket per team, and two rounds of High Explosive ammunition from the Carl Gustavs should get us the result we needed. I decided to save my snipers' weapons and ammunition to engage targets of opportunity once we had regained the initiative.

It was possible, I knew, that I would have to 'starburst' the platoon, and order an escape and evasion. The idea was simmering in the back of my mind.

The only position I wasn't able to reach was the sentry: he was cut off, and I feared he was already dead. I'd have to deal with that possibility when we got to it, but for now we just had to repel this attack and survive the rest of the day.

———

How did a guy like me get himself into this calamity? And what did I take away from the experience?

Well, that's what this book is about. I'm going to share with you stories from my career as a soldier and an officer, but I'll also be describing what I've learnt about resilience, optimisation, leadership and values, and how to create high-performing teams. Some of the lessons were hard won, and others were thrust on me by my superiors. Together, they made me the man I am today.

RESILIENCE

1

GIVE YOURSELF NO OTHER OPTION

'The difference between imposed discipline and
self-discipline is only the person imposing it.'

Very early in my long journey to becoming a Special Forces soldier,
I learnt that if you want something bad enough, you have to commit
to it fully. You must put all your eggs in one basket. Especially if what
you're trying to achieve is truly difficult—if it's against the odds or at
the extremities of your capabilities—you can't give yourself any other
option. Your focus must be only on your goal. Total commitment
is essential.

When I was in Year 10 at school in South Australia all I talked
about was joining the Army. Early on, I had dreams of being an officer.
The chivalry, honour, sense of duty—these were all traits of my heroes
of the day. I watched the TV show *Tour of Duty* religiously, and it
was the clean-cut young lieutenant and the burly and wise platoon
sergeant who sparked my interest in leadership. They espoused a
type of yin and yang approach to managing men in combat. Years
later, in Afghanistan, I would have a very similar relationship with
my platoon sergeant, Paul Cale.

On the weekends I made out I was the platoon commander.
I dressed in Army greens and went into the bush to fight my friends
with slingshots. In Year 11, though, I wasn't getting the grades
I would need if I was to become an officer. I was interested in study,

and I wasn't stupid, but I was falling behind and couldn't keep up with the smarter kids in the class, especially three girls who seemed to be breezing their way through the study. I tried desperately to keep up with one in particular. She was my first crush and we dated on and off, but her smarts never washed off on me.

Looking back now, I see that I wasn't managing my time efficiently, and I didn't know how to study for the things that were most important. Purpose and interest were always my reasons for not doing well in certain subjects. I was shithouse at maths because I couldn't see the purpose. If there's such a thing as dyslexia for numbers, I probably have it. It didn't help that my teacher had the personality of the board he wrote on. Yet I excelled at economics, because the teacher explained it in terms I understood: 'Imagine this is your money . . .'

It didn't help either that I had an inferiority complex when it came to my father. This was no fault of his. Fathers often say things that affect their sons for years to come—after all, they're not really trained for the job. Dad tried to get me to study harder by telling me I could never become a fireman like him with the grades that I was getting. This was a tough thing to hear given that, as well as Dad, my grandfather on Mum's side and my uncle were both fireys. As well, I saw a career as an infantry officer in the Army as an even harder thing to achieve, so all I heard was that I'd never make it to the Royal Military College with my grades. I clearly remember the moment I realised that if I wanted to join the Army, I would have to look at general enlistment.

At the start of Year 12, I was still only sixteen—too young to enlist. I dropped out a few weeks in and drifted around for the best part of ten months, working on sheep stations and willing time to speed up. My seventeenth birthday felt like a lifetime away, but finally I was old enough to march into the Defence Force Recruiting Office in Adelaide. I applied, was accepted and then waited another three months for my enlistment date.

There was a brief swearing-in ceremony at the Defence Force Recruiting Office, then we were asked to meet at the train station. My family had come to see me off, and as the train began its journey to Melbourne on 2 February 1991, I felt relief wash over me: I was leaving them behind. That should have made it clear to me that I wasn't happy at home. In fact, I was lonely, and now I was off on the adventure of a lifetime, with nothing but opportunity ahead of me. Or so I thought.

I had been sworn in as Recruit Connolly, making my oath to the Queen. The corporal career advisor travelled with us to Melbourne on the overnight train. My only real memories of this trip were sitting there listening to my new mate Travis telling me about his time in the reserves, and him and the corporal sharing a few jokes. Jokes you'd only understand if you'd been there. Already I felt out of my depth.

The next morning, I found myself on a coach arriving at Kapooka, the 'home' of the soldier. When we pulled up, a couple of people jumped on and started yelling at us to get off, and to 'move like we meant it'. One thing that has not and will never change is the need for recruits to sense the 'shock of capture'. It was a profound moment for us all.

We were sorted into two lines and hustled down the road, being yelled at all the way to keep our 'fucking head and eyes to the front'. A senior platoon marched by us: they were in parade uniforms, ironed to a crisp, they seemed to all be the same height and they walked tall as they marched past, staring straight ahead. A sergeant walked at the back of the other crew, chanting, ''Eft, 'ight, 'eft, 'ight, 'eft, 'ight . . .' These soldiers' arms and legs moved as one; ours jostled each other, and we even sometimes tripped up the person next to us. They looked proud, whereas we looked like a beaten butcher's dog.

We were assembled in front of the quartermaster's store. This is the primary building for the issuing and receipt of all the items a soldier needs to do their job. One by one we were ushered in and told we had to sign for a green canvas bag containing all manner of stuff. We were ordered to change into a green tracksuit and a pair of Dunlop KT26 runners.

The men out the front were receiving another lesson, known as 'Hurry up and wait'. In the Army, every soldier learns that you rush at the start of something, and then wait around for ages for something to happen. It's not an intentional lesson, but patience is a valuable skill—one sadly missing from the kids of today.

Once we were all assembled with our green canvas bags, we were marched to the 'hairdresser'. I sat and looked in the mirror. The young man looking back at me had a thick mop of shiny dark brown hair, parted in the middle in the style of the time. He was fresh-faced and innocent. I was asked how I'd like my hair cut, and I was starting to answer when the clippers went straight through the centre of my hair in a deep shave. I'm sure that joke never got old. Seven more solid blows of the shears and I was suddenly a skinny kid with a shaved head. I felt like my identity had been stolen.

Only many years later, when I was the officer in charge of selection, did I understand the importance of prioritising your existential worth over your external projections. People use the way they present themselves to the world as armour, and they hide behind it. I now know the psychological impact that the first head shave has on a young man who joins the Army. It has broken more than a few. It broke me. I was suddenly terrified: this shit had just got very fucking real.

With our hair removed, we were shown to our new rooms, where we had 30 minutes to unpack our gear and organise it exactly as shown on the laminated picture hanging on the back of the door. We rushed to get it done. The shock of capture had well and truly been achieved, but there was so much more to come

———

Thirteen Platoon was to be my home for the next three months. Our motto was 'Unlucky for Some'. That was certainly true for some—a few guys dropped out along the way—but for me the number thirteen has always been a very lucky one.

The next morning I was taught to shave, even though there was not a hair on my face to miss. The smell of lime Gillette shaving cream still triggers a surge of emotion in me, and I find myself shaving at a rapid rate. The time to get in and out of the ablutions was measured to the second, and enforced. We were kids playing soldiers, even then.

I was shouted at from sunup to sundown, and sometimes in the middle of the night.

'Get out in the hallway!'

'Get out of the hallway!'

'Where's your cutlery?'

'Do you call that clean?'

'Your socks look sad!' the corporal would scream, his mouth inches away from my ear, while throwing a pair out the second-storey window. 'Go down and get your socks, and they'd better be fucking happy when they get back in the drawer!'

The emotional wellbeing of my socks was a very serious issue indeed, so I turned up the corners of the socks as much as possible. Finally they sat in my drawer beaming back at the corporal.

'Do you think you're smarter than me?' he loved to roar at us.

That was one of my favourites, because deep down I probably did think I was smarter than him.

'No, corporal!' I'd shout back, in unison with the other recruits.

The second week and third week weren't much easier than the first: there was more shouting, beds overturned and lockers emptied on the floor, with a personal weapon thrown into the mix. My stress levels went through the roof.

Meals were rushed. Jostling at one side of the mess hall, we would pile food high onto our plates while being yelled at to go faster. Fighting for space at a table, we huddled over our brown stewy slop, holding our cutlery as much as for defence as to eat. Three mouthfuls in, we'd be shouted at: 'Get out on parade!' Then it was a quick sprint with the others for the door and we'd stand in line for inspection. If we were lucky, this would happen during dessert.

I realised early on that I could steal food for later. Call it the Anzac spirit, or maybe it was some Australian convict heritage shining through, but I would shove bananas, apples, cake or bread into my pockets. My smuggling career was going swimmingly until the second week, when I was sprung during a snap inspection not long after we had gone to bed. I had forgotten a piece of chocolate cake that I had wrapped in a napkin and dropped into the drawer of my bedside table.

I stood rigid to attention by my bed, with my sheet over my left arm and my counterpane over my right. Bombardier Dix looked at me and smiled—the first time I'd seen him do this. Unable to fault my locker presentation, he went over to my bedside table and opened the drawer. My eyes darted left. *Shit* . . . I had forgotten about the cake. I was about to be the central figure in a scene reminiscent of the movie *Full Metal Jacket*, when Private Pile is caught with a jelly doughnut in his footlocker.

'What on fucken' earth is this then?' he asked, looking at me. At six foot three, he was an imposing figure.

'Cake, Bombardier.' I racked my brain for an excuse.

'Cake!' he screamed. 'Cake! Hallway Thirteen,' he yelled, 'Recruit Connolly likes chocolate cake! Don't you, recruit?'

'Yes, Bombadier,' I yelled, as the rest of the platoon ran from their rooms.

'So, Recruit Connolly is going to eat this cake, and all of you are going to do push-ups while he does. Each time you get to ten he will take a bite. Do you all understand?'

'Yes, Bombadier!' the men yelled.

They dropped to their hands and knees and started doing push-ups, yelling the cadence together. I took a bite at ten—though I wasn't smart enough to shove the whole thing in my mouth. They got to ten more and I took another bite and chewed. *This isn't so bad*, I thought. *The guys will be fine—I just fucked up.*

They pumped out another ten, then another, while I ate my cake. They had got to 100 or so by the time I took the final bite. I looked along the hallway at the murderous glances directed my way. I had just received an introduction to group punishments. The guys didn't talk to me for a few days, but over time they seemed to forget—or so I thought.

———

It was when we did physical training, especially running, that I came into my own. Only a year ago I had finished second in the interschool athletics carnival for the 800 metres, and third in the 1500 metres. So I had an engine. As well as being able to hold thresholds for a long period, I could also sprint, which stood me in good stead.

There was a set of steps carved into the hill behind the gym, and often for punishment we would have to run up the hill and around the lone tree. It was about 400 metres all up, and I was usually first or not far off the pace. Occasionally our physical training instructor would yell after us, 'Anyone who doesn't beat Recruit Connolly will have to go around again.' That would make me run all the faster.

I was hated for this, but I didn't know it. If I could go back in time and talk to young Recruit Connolly, I'd take him aside and tell him to stop being an arsehole. But no one had that quiet word with me and I carried on oblivious.

Over time the distances we were made to run increased—from 400 to 600 to 800 metres, up and down this grassy hill. I would shadow the other guys, wait for the last 200 and then kick into gear; I was playing with them. Many guys in my platoon suffered and ran up that hill more times than they had to because I couldn't resist the competition of the other guys. I regret that behaviour now.

The platoon staff were great, if I'm honest, and I look back on them with fondness. When the shouting finally stopped and they started to warm to us—because we recruits had learnt that self-discipline is easier than the alternative—we started to click as a cohesive team. We did small field trips to learn the basics of Army tactics, which I loved, and there was weapons training, which I didn't care much for back then. I just liked being out bush.

Given the way I behaved at first when I was a recruit at Kapooka, it probably won't come as a surprise that I was bullied. I didn't realise it was bullying back then, though; I thought it was just that some guys in the platoon didn't like me. That's the way the world was, I figured: you can't be friends with everyone.

I had a smart mouth and would call people out if they deserved it, and one night I called out the wrong guy. He and two of his mates decided to sneak into my room at night with bars of soap in socks and belt the shit out of me. I tried to fight back but realised I couldn't win, so I simply curled up on my bed and took it.

I cried myself to sleep that night, and I thought about quitting. At times like that I really hated the place. But I had told so many people that I was joining the Army, and I'd passed up lots of other opportunities to be here, so I couldn't just quit. I hated my home life too and didn't want to go back there. I had no other option but to stay. I also decided that nothing was going to stop me from finishing Kapooka.

Those three guys didn't come near me again. I've often wondered where they ended up. In the early years I thought a lot about finding them and dealing with them on my terms. Then, as I matured, I started to see it as a life lesson. I reasoned that, to a degree, I'd brought it on myself, and that I should have thought more carefully about how I interacted with them. I learnt that not every interaction, physical or otherwise, needs to be combative. If I came across those guys now, I might even buy them a beer for the lesson they gave me.

As time went on, I came to love the experience of Kapooka, and I was very proud when I marched out of there. In the years that followed, it became a frame of reference for me. The key lesson I took was not to give myself an out. I wouldn't truly understand this until I failed the selection course for the Special Air Service Regiment (SASR). Only by then had I gained the introspection that allowed me to see what Kapooka had taught me.

My uncle and my cousin came to watch me in our final March Out Parade which was great. I never really expected Dad and Mum to come, as Kapooka is so far away from Adelaide. But now that I have my own sons, I don't really understand why Dad didn't come. He remained an enigma to me throughout my life—to the day he died, if I'm honest. In some ways, though, his emotional absence helped shape me and I can only assume that it is also the reason I wasn't easily affected when I witnessed death during my deployments.

I also know now that I would have made a great firefighter too.

LESSONS

It's human nature to want to take the easy option when it presents itself. But to get what you want in life, you need to apply yourself and do the hard yards. Never fear the tough option.

Do put all your eggs in one basket.

Aim as high as you can imagine. The worst that can happen is you make it only some of the way.

Strive for the things you dream of, even if they're things your peers can't or won't do. You don't need their permission.

You don't have to win every race; in fact, sometimes it's better to let others win.

2

LAZINESS CAN QUICKLY BECOME A HABIT

'Practice does not make perfect. Only perfect
practice makes perfect.'

Vince Lombardi, NFL head coach

Fast-forward about a year. It's October 1992 and I'm in the 1st Battalion as a forward scout, and we're in the jungle. The jungle has an amazing ability to amplify a person's laziness, and I was about to learn a major lesson: good habits take time and effort to develop, but bad habits seem to creep up on us and take over our lives.

I read somewhere once that 'practice makes perfect, so be careful what you practise'. This rings especially true for laziness. If you get into a habit of taking short cuts, it quickly becomes your default setting.

Nothing comes easy. Yes, humans are creatures of habit. But we're also, by nature, lazy as shit. Energy preservation is an innate part of human survival. But some of our habits develop and stick because we quite simply can't be fucked to do more than the absolute minimum—so we develop a habit of minimal effort. In short, being dedicated to improving yourself, professionally or physically, is a habit that must be practised.

The jungle is hot and wet: some can hit 39 degrees Celsius, at 95 per cent humidity. Unless you've felt the weight and asphyxiating heat of what I'm sure is hell on earth, it's a sensation that is difficult to describe. Even breathing feels laboured: it's like cling wrap has been tightly wound around your chest. Your lungs are constricted by nothing other than the sky you're under. And if you're not sweating from the humidity, you're being rained on.

There are usually swarms of insects around you, all attracted to your face. You inhale some with every breath, while others crawl down the back of your muddy, sweaty neck and into your shirt. The plants have thorns or spines, and if you try to fight them away they tear at your uniform until they get access to your skin, and then they tear at that too. It takes huge amounts of self-discipline not to panic, not to fight the environment. It feels like everything here wants to kill you.

Plants get nicknames like 'the fuck-you tree', which looks like a small and plump palm tree—except all the branches have three-inch long thorns on them. I remember firing and moving through the jungle one time, popping up and dropping back down as I went. I had the M72A6 66-millimetre rocket launcher slung across my back as I sprinted past a fuck-you tree. As I ducked to avoid one of these thorny branches, it caught the 66 sticking out from my back. The branch was whipped into my neck, and my forward momentum took care of the rest. Every single thorn on this fucking branch embedded itself in my neck.

The pressing heat and humidity can also give you prickly heat. This starts at your eyebrows and works its way to your heels. After a while, it changes from being slightly uncomfortable to painful, and then severely painful the longer it is left unchecked. Imagine a pain so severe it feels like you're covered in acupuncture needles, but they're all on fire and actually touching your bones. The only time it goes away is when you remain still and stop sweating, which rarely happens.

The fact that this kind of pain is always present is emotionally draining. And there's nothing you can do to make it stop, because the only thing that gets rid of it is being clean and taking hot showers for a number of days. I've seen some hard men near to tears because they've had prickly heat for several weeks. It takes all your self-control to remain calm. I can only imagine what those in the Vietnam War must have felt. The jungle sucks bad enough in training, so actual jungle warfare must be hell; I take my hat off to those who lived it for years on end.

So, in late October 1992 I was on an exercise at the Jungle Warfare Training Centre near Tully, in Far North Queensland. We had one last exercise to do as a company, and the field trip seemed to coincide with the early arrival of the wet season. My section had been leading the company through the thick Koombooloomba scrub and jungle. I was the forward scout and everything was pulling at my clothes, biting my skin and irritating me. I led us onto a small hill in the jungle and towards a clearing where we would take up an overwatch position within the company harbour location.

We crept through the low vegetation and silently took our positions. The idea was to lie in silence for a few minutes and tune in to our surroundings: if an enemy force had followed us, or if an enemy position was close by, we might hear them before they heard us. We lay there silently, covered in sweat from hacking through a hard stretch of lantana, and then from carrying our packs up the large hill. Fortunately for me, I weighed only 55 kilograms, and my pack and webbing added another 10 kilograms.

When I say we were covered in sweat, I mean we were absolutely sodden. I watched as the steam rose from my arms and hands, and the mosquitoes were drawn to the heat signature. Jungle mosquitoes are huge. Watching someone else encounter them can be entertaining, as they're surrounded by what looks like a small dark cloud. But the small dark cloud is made up of mosquitoes, all of them hungry for blood. If they could organise themselves, they'd probably be strong enough to carry a small man away.

Five minutes later, we slowly rose from the wet ground and went about our business. The platoon commander sited the main gun pit positions around the defensive perimeter. He then sited two more forward weapon pits, linking to the main machine gun pit in the next section. Lastly, he sited his own weapon pit in depth with one of the scouts.

'Hoochies', or simple tents, were erected between trees and then lowered to ground level until nightfall. A track plan was established between the section weapon pits, and communications cord set up around the perimeter and into the centre of the defensive position, linking all the weapon pits. The overnight security piquet, or watch, would be maintained at the main section gun pit.

We started little hexamine solid fuel fires and had a cup of tea and a can of food. The section commander retrieved the sentry and I was summoned to go out on a clearing patrol of the area to the front of our position to ensure there were no enemy in the immediate vicinity. I returned and we had another period of silence as we waited for darkness to fall.

We were now into the night routine, and I went to my shelter and slowly started to get out of my webbing and wet clothes. I undid the garbage bag that contained my dry clothes and got changed. The aim was to keep your sleeping bag dry for as long as possible, and the only way to do that was to climb into it in a dry uniform. I hung out my wet uniform on one of the lines that secured my hoochie to the tree.

I woke during the night to the sound of rain hammering on my shelter. It absolutely thundered down, as it can do only in the jungle. I lay there, dry and warm in my sleeping bag, listening to the water falling from the heavens. This was my second year in the battalion, and despite the mosquitoes biting my sweaty hands, this was one of the things I loved most about deploying into the field. I fell asleep again and was woken later for my piquet. I rolled over and looked outside, and could see clear sky and stars through a large hole in the canopy. *Awesome*, I thought. *Sometimes you just get looked after.*

I rolled up my sleeping bag to stop any scorpions, spiders or other jungle creatures from taking up residence in it. I had rolled my socks over the entrance to my boots before going to bed with much the same idea. With my boots and webbing now on, and with my rifle in hand, I made my way to the piquet.

My section commander was Murray, a spritely and at times angry little man. He took one look at me and grunted his disapproval. 'You're a fucking idiot.'

'What?' I replied.

'You've been around long enough to know that you don't wear your dry cams on piquet.'

I thought about this for a moment and was annoyed at him for not letting me make my own decisions without chastising me.

'Haven't you learnt anything?' Murray continued. 'Or do you think you know better than me?'

'No, I just saw stars out, and it's only for an hour,' I protested. 'Surely I can be trusted to make my own decisions on when I put on my own uniform?'

'Well, let's see how this works out for you then, smart-arse.'

As if on cue, the mist rolled in and it started to spit. Murray always seemed to have an incredible ability to have an 'I told you so' moment. As the rain's intensity increased, Murray's smile widened. He sat there, already sodden, and didn't take his eyes off me. My uniform was slowly getting darker as it became wetter.

Murray slapped me on one saturated shoulder as he got up. 'I think we're gonna be bumped by the enemy before sunrise, Conno. Keep that in mind, cobber.' He walked away, leaving me looking like a drowned rat—the way I should have looked at the start of the sentry duty, had I donned my wet uniform as I'd been taught.

The rain fell all through my piquet duty. I lay there in silence, then went to wake the machine gunner for his shift. I returned to my shelter and looked at my other set of wet cams hanging on my hoochie. What to do now? If I got in my sleeping bag for the last hour before we were due to rise, my sleeping bag would get wet. I couldn't strip off and get in there; if we were bumped by the enemy, I'd never be able to pack my gear and get my wet uniform on fast enough, and could be left behind.

Slowly I started to pack my gear. I changed out of my fresh, wet cams and put the old sweaty and dirty ones back on. They stank. I might have had wet cams in my pack, but at least they weren't wet *and* dirty.

I saw Murray the next morning, but I wasn't mature enough to understand that this was the time I should tell him what I'd learnt from my mistake. Instead, I kept a low profile for a few days. He was a great non-commissioned officer, or NCO, and I vowed not to let him down again—or myself, for that matter—by being lazy.

————

'Prior preparation prevents piss-poor performance.' It's an old saying, but it's also linked to not being lazy in the first place. Good basic soldiering is about not being lazy. Similar principles apply in the Arctic, in the jungle and in temperate woodlands. The skills and drills you're taught can mean survival, but mostly they mean combat efficiency.

Mistakes like the one I made are important, but leaders don't always understand that correcting such errors has to be about the superordinate goal. Bad leaders simply see an opportunity to discipline someone, in the way they were once disciplined, but they're not thinking about *why*. Having a warm and dry set of clothes and sleeping bag isn't about being comfortable. The superordinate goal is to keep soldiers efficient and operating at the highest level possible, given the circumstances. A soldier who hasn't slept properly will be tired and less able to concentrate. They will miss cues and combat indicators, and be less alert when it comes to contact. They'll also start making small mistakes.

Enforcing discipline and dispelling laziness isn't just something NCOs do because they want to be a hardarse and smash anyone who doesn't obey their orders. It's because the more disciplined their soldiers are, the more effective they will be in battle. Not being lazy in the little things means that you and others will be less dead during the big things.

One of the best leaders I ever worked for phrased this perfectly. 'I don't give a fuck if you're well rested, fed and comfortable,' he told me. 'But when we get into the shit, I need to know you're operating at as close to 100 per cent as possible. If you're not applying your skills and drills like you've been taught, you're deducting from that 100 per cent at a rapid rate. If I ever catch you at 95 per cent, I'll fuck you up.'

The lesson stuck, and not being lazy has saved my life on more than one occasion since then.

Some six years later, I was on the mountain warfare course in the back of the Victorian snow country. It was a particularly nasty snow season in 1998, with arctic like temperatures and snap blizzards. I was lying in my tent at night and felt the need to go to the bathroom. But it was early morning and there was still quality sleep to be had. I thought back to Murray and the lesson I'd learnt about laziness.

If I decided not to get up and go to the toilet, I knew, I wouldn't be able to sleep anymore. The mountains are an arduous environment, and being well rested and nourished helps you contend with the cold and the effects of high altitude. Also, I was in a thick, goose-down sleeping bag and yet I was shivering; I also knew that if you have to go to the toilet in a cold environment, your body diverts warmth from the extremities to keep the urine warm. This means you're unnecessarily spending valuable energy on a bodily function, and that you become cold faster anyway. In the same way, holding in a shit will dehydrate you faster as your body diverts fluids to stop your turd from turning into a brick.

In normal life we don't think that minor discomforts can be life-threatening. But exposure kills. The Arctic is unforgiving, and when you're pushing yourself physically every day, the little things can become big things. Losing a glove may mean losing the hand it was supposed to be on. Not eating enough can mean hypothermia and death.

For a soldier, the simple act of not consuming a full Arctic ration pack like you're supposed to—about 6000 calories—means your body does not have the fuel to warm itself in an emergency. There are guys who still lose weight on double rations in the Arctic. Fuel equals warmth, and warmth isn't just comfortable—it keeps you alive. Getting wet in the Arctic is a life-threatening emergency.

I rolled over, willing myself to get out of bed. The arguments played out in my mind, and finally I sat up and unzipped the sleeping bag. I was met by air so cold it took my breath away.

I opened the tent and grabbed my boots, jamming my feet in them fast, and then slipped on some woollen gloves. I had almost fallen into the deep snow by the time I was dressed. I relieved myself (remember, never eat the yellow snow!) and then reversed the process. A few minutes later I was back in my sleeping bag; although I was shivering, I could feel myself warming up. I was sound asleep within minutes, and a few hours later got up feeling refreshed and ready for the day. The importance of not being lazy was reinforced for me.

Also relevant is the fact that being lazy has compounding effects. I might have got away with it on this night in the mountains. I might have been awake for a few hours and then had some broken sleep. The days on the mountain warfare course are strenuous: there's lots of cross-country skiing, which is exhausting, and made more so by the heavy pack and military equipment you carry. If you don't get adequate sleep, your exhaustion is compounded. The more fatigued you become, the harder tasks get. The less sleep you have, the more fatigue sets in and the lazier you become.

The circle isn't usually complete until you make a decision—or, more likely, fail to make a decision—to take a hard right over an easy wrong. I once watched a commando start to remove his metal tent pins from the freezing snow. He could have walked the five feet to his pack and put on his inner gloves, but he was lazy and just began pulling out the stakes. Freezing metal on warm skin is dangerous—as he realised as soon as he grasped the metal shard and it stuck fast to his hand.

We had to use warm water to try to bring his hand and the metal pin to the same temperature, before separating them. The pin came away, along with most of the skin on his palm. He needed first aid, and was left with a painful reminder for the duration of the course and beyond about the importance of not being lazy. In my experience, when someone injures themselves as a result of laziness, it's usually the tip of the iceberg. Other short cuts will have been taken.

———

We can take heart from the fact that once we've identified that we have the tendency to be lazy, there's a strategy we can implement to counteract this. It's as simple as telling yourself that you're being lazy. It's important to visualise the second-order effects of your laziness, and the problems that you're creating for yourself or others by the behaviour. After an event that didn't work out well for you as a result of laziness, focus on identifying the lazy behaviour and reflect on the negative consequence of taking the easy wrong over the hard right.

It was no accident that I learnt these lessons out of necessity, operating in harsh environments. The jungle and the snow will kill the unprepared person within days, and will make life a misery for the prepared person who is lazy. Our modern city lives are very sheltered, and lazy people can operate with relative ease—until they're in an environment they can't control.

Don't make laziness your habit.

LESSONS

Survival is human nature, and one of our strongest subconscious urges. Energy conservation is a large component of this. It makes us want to expend as little energy as possible, often by taking the lazy option. Discipline means overriding this urge, in order to achieve subordinate and superordinate goals.

Getting away with a lazy option more than once creates bad habits; don't let that happen. Bad habits can be reprogrammed, but doing so is infinitely harder than preventing them from developing.

Always think of ways to work smarter, not harder.

3

THE ADVANTAGE OF FEAR

'Being on the edge isn't as safe,
but the view is better.'

Ricky Gervais

Fear is a natural extension of not being lazy: it's hard to be lazy when you're scared, and you can't be lazy if you're going to face your fears. The Army is good at reminding us of that.

I wasn't a particularly brave child: I was scared of the usual things. When I was in primary school in Adelaide back in the 1980s, a few high-profile child abduction and murder cases were reported on the TV news, and for a while I was terrified at night that someone would pull me through the window. The sounds of hoons doing burnouts at 3 am would not only wake me, but also have me deep under the covers, my imagination running wild.

I was about fifteen when I stopped being scared of most things—except for clowns, thanks to Stephen King; I won't ever be comfortable around those freaky bastards. But the scariest moment I experienced in the Army came early in my career, and it was also a revelation.

———

Somalia, 1993. I cautiously edged closer to the shallow creek line, scanning the foreground for enemy activity. I felt like I was being watched. My heart rate increased, the hairs stood up on the back of my neck and I shivered involuntarily. This had happened to me a few times during my jungle warfare training in Tully. It was fear, but it wasn't the same as being scared. My senses were in overdrive, and I felt that contact was imminent.

The morning was warm. It was around 8 am and we'd been patrolling for more than an hour. The sun was rising rapidly behind me. I half-slid, half-stepped down a sandy embankment, and as I moved, I thought I saw something a few hundred metres up the hill, on the other side of the wadi, or dry riverbed. I got to the bottom of the creek and sprinted hard for about 20 metres. Another scout also entered the creek, going the other way. Brett and I worked well together: we knew each other's actions and reactions without saying a word.

I popped up and fixed my eyes on the area where I thought I'd seen something. I could just make out what looked like a person lying on the ground below one of the many camel thorn bushes that lined the gentle slope. The bush this guy was hiding under was among a few larger trees, their small branches manicured to a standard height by the passing camels.

The enemy had spotted me and Brett exiting the creek from our different locations, so he needed to change his sight picture. I saw a sudden flash of light as he did, and Brett saw it too. I assumed it was a reflection from his rifle scope, and I hit the ground. 'Contact front!' I yelled.

The distance between us was about 400 metres; as I crawled to take up a site picture, I saw the Somali get up and run from behind his bush, making serious speed to the crest and then over the back of the hill.

My section commander demanded a target indication. I scanned the area for a moment and then looked at Brett, who had taken up a position in line with me, about 20 metres away.

He raised his eyebrows and smiled. 'What ya got?' he asked.

'I think he was over there somewhere,' I replied, pointing to a group of trees and bushes. 'What do you think?'

'I'm not sure—he was gone pretty fast.'

I felt confident there was no threat anymore; Brett was one of the best scouts I ever worked with, and I trusted his judgement. He was a great soldier and I was lucky to have him as a mentor.

Standing, I made my way back to the section commander. The hairs on the back of my neck were down now, and I was relaxed as I told him I had seen the reflection of a scope and then someone had run off. He eyed me dubiously, and suggested we take a closer look.

I led us towards the cluster of bushes, although they all looked the same as we started up the hill. I was sure he'd run off without his gun. We searched for it for fifteen minutes or so but found nothing, and I began to feel like an idiot.

'We need to get going, mate,' the section commander suggested a further ten minutes later.

'I know it's around here somewhere.' I scanned the surrounding areas, all the places we'd looked ten times already, in the hope that the rifle would magically appear.

'I believe you, but we have to conduct a marry-up with the rest of the platoon, and at this rate they'll be waiting for us for hours.'

I knew the boss wasn't confident about what I claimed I'd seen, and I was now getting dirty looks from the other guys in the section. I was the youngest and most junior soldier in the section, and I had a reputation as a smart-arse pretty boy with a big mouth. Understandably, I wasn't everyone's favourite.

I reluctantly obeyed and headed off with Brett as directed. We moved silently up the slope in an arrowhead formation. Whoever had been lying under the bushes had long gone, but I was still looking for some footprints at least. I hadn't found anything, and was about to give up.

The camel thorn bushes channelled me into a narrow track that had been used by animals. It was a minor obstacle, so I needed to be covered. I looked over my shoulder to make sure the section commander had seen the direction I was heading. As I moved around a small bush, I tripped over a branch. When I pulled my foot from under it and steadied myself, I realised the branch was actually a rifle that had been covered with leaves. And not just any rifle—it was an M1 Garand fitted with a scope.

The M1 Garand is a US Armed Forces rifle of World War Two vintage. It was supplied to a number of US allies to aid in Foreign Internal Defence (FID), so it was no surprise to see one fitted with a scope turn up in the Horn of Africa.

The young militiaman had been watching me, I realised, and he'd been startled by my appearance at a different location than he was expecting. The scouting techniques I had been taught may well have saved my life. He not only chose not to fire at me—he fled without taking his rifle.

I called over my section commander and we studied the rifle. The safety catch was off and it was in excellent condition. We didn't know about preserving evidence back then—this was just a rifle—so we cleared it and carried it out with us. We had been searching about 100 metres too close, near where we had exited the creek bed (an easy mistake to make when judging distances up an incline, and when the vegetation is similar across the observable area). I had been lucky. A combination of fear and training is a powerful thing.

———

My fears are different now. They focus on the safety and education of my children, and the protection, both emotional and physical, of my wife. These things are important to me and keep me awake more than worries about my personal wellbeing. As we get older, our fears change.

I've learnt to be comfortable while scared, and that's because I've been exposed to my fears, continuously and incrementally. I'm not comfortable working at heights but I'm not terrified either, although I do get scared being too close to the edge of a building or cliff.

About ten minutes' drive out of the centre of Nowra, on the South Coast of New South Wales, is an inland Royal Australian Navy base called HMAS Albatross. Part of the base, but in a separate compound, is the Army's Parachute Training School (PTS). There's a saying at the PTS: 'Knowledge dispels fear.' Understanding what fear is helps you not only to overcome it, but also to perform better when it really counts. Fear lives in the dark recesses of our minds, and even visiting these places once can dispel our fear of what they hold.

When I finished the commando course, I was required to do the parachute course; my future in Special Forces relied on it. I visualised being successful on this course for months beforehand. When it began, I concentrated harder on the techniques than I had for any other course. I listened to the instructors, studied hard and thought about their motto. *Knowledge dispels fear.*

We were exposed to the 'risers' first: we'd be suspended off the ground and conduct parachuting flight drills. Then we moved on to the towers, and it was here that I experienced vertigo. I'd get to the edge of the tower and, hooked up to the wire and suspended in my harness, I would jump off. My landings were never pretty because my eyes would be closed when my feet hit the ground. This was clearly something I needed to work on: I had to learn to function properly while terrified.

When the time came for our first jump, I experienced sensory overload. The red light was on and we yelled out our equipment checks. I mumbled something under my breath while the rest of the line of men, known in parachuting as the 'Stick', shuffled towards the door. The green light came on and the loadmaster screamed, 'Go!'

The first guy went, and I shuffled forward. Then the next—'Go! ... Go! ... Go!' And then I was at the door. I think the loadmaster just got out the 'G', and I was gone. It was so noisy, and then instantly quiet.

I went through my count as my body was thrown around in the wash of the C-130 Hercules' engines. 'One thousand, two thousand, three...' My chute's canopy opened and I was jerked out of my freefall. 'Thank fuck for that!' I yelled, feeling obliged to let the universe know how grateful I was. I would repeat this call on every jump I ever did.

How did I get through it? In my mind I had decided that this was it—suicide almost. I had resolved that I was comfortable taking my life in my hands and just jumping out the door. I didn't understand back then that I'd made a slow progression to this point—increments of exposure that allowed me to build my resilience.

I'm still not a great parachutist, but if the canopy opens, I'm happy. I've jumped a lot of times, many of them into water, following boats that have been bundled into the ocean. There was a time when this was one of the main capabilities of commandos, and we practised it every few months. There's a lot to think about, which can take your mind off the jump and the height. But for me there's no escaping the fear I feel when the ramp of a C-130 Hercules, or occasionally a DHC-4 Caribou, was lowered. But it was manageable. The fear made me braver.

———

Confronting my fear of heights took me to a crazy new level (so to speak). You see, I'm also a lead rock climber. I trained in this not long after the parachute course, partly because I wanted to conquer my fear and partly because it was a niche specialty that few others were training in.

To be a good rock climber, you must be technically competent and you must be brave. It can kill you in a number of ways, and you need to know how to mitigate the risks. But at the end of the day, gravity is always there, waiting for you to put a foot or a hand in the wrong place. I like to refer to it as a slow chaos.

I've led a few climbs over the years, and established ropes and ladders for the roping supervisors to guide the company up a cliff assault. I've climbed buildings and ships and wharfs and rocks. I loved climbing, but I hated it more. There's no doubt in my mind that any courage I displayed in combat was a result of genetics, stupidity and testing myself through climbing when I was in my twenties. (Mainly stupidity, if I'm honest.)

I started out as a soldier being scared of several things, but my fear could perhaps be better described as a healthy respect for those things. Not being lazy gave me the drive to understand my attitude. Knowledge dispels fear. I found that I was able to challenge my fears, overcome them in the short term, and in some cases master them for life.

LESSONS

Having a healthy respect for danger is a good thing. Knowledge can dispel fear, but it can't take it away entirely. Nor should it.

Fear has its place. It exists to keep us alive.

Identify when fear is making you perform better and when it makes you worse. Then work to discard the components of fear that limit you.

Lessons, drills, procedures and processes will help you to do things automatically, so that you don't worry about your ability to carry them out. Exposure to an intimidating environment will give you the confidence you need to operate there.

Being oblivious to a danger can lull us into a false sense of security, often resulting in poor or unconsidered decisions that affect not just ourselves but also those around us.

4

MATESHIP IS A POWERFUL ASSET

'The thing I can't stand about you mate is you're
always so bloody cheerful.'

Mel Gibson as Frank Dunne, *Gallipoli*, 1981

Our relationships define us and protect us. Of all the lessons I learnt
in the Army, this is the most important. The power of mateship can't
be understated. Understanding how soldiers interact with each other
and how teams coalesce was pivotal to my success as a junior leader
and, later, as a platoon commander in combat.

To my mind, friendship and mateship are different. Friendships
form when we meet others who have similar interests to us and share
our values. Mateship is more than this: it's a stronger bond, and is
forged through some level of adversity.

In order to build a high-performing team, military commanders
have to create environments in which mateship can be cultivated.
They do this by developing challenging and realistic training scenarios, by testing individuals to their personal limits, and by ensuring
that teams work at their collective best. Mateship is born through
sharing arduous conditions, enduring the same hardships and, ultimately, enjoying shared successes. It also arises naturally through
operational service, especially combat missions, where a unit builds
a collective sense of purpose.

For friendship to evolve into mateship in civilian life, friends
rely on experiential learning—about themselves and one another.

Such experiences can have the same characteristics as combat, if less intensely, but mateship takes longer to emerge.

———

Townsville, circa 2000. I could just hear the three-minute call echoing around the back of the ageing MC-130 Talon aircraft from the US Air Force Special Operations Command. I rose from my orange netting seat, squinting my eyes in the dim red light. Steadying myself against the changing speed of the old aircraft, I gave my equipment the first of many cursory checks. A reduction in speed and a change of pitch in the engines was always a sign that we were entering the run into the drop zone. It's also the most dangerous time for the ageing aircraft, as it must slow to just above stalling speed to allow the parachutists to jump. Everything was going well.

Behind me in the aircraft, the lads were doing last-minute checks of their dry bags and reserve parachutes. Leaning on the edge of the seats, I adjusted the fins secured to my feet, making sure they were tight around the back of my jungle boots. I felt for the knife that was secured to my calf and heaved the heavy dry bag—which contained my pack, webbing and weapon—up off the floor, bending over to secure the weight against my legs. I checked that my lowering line was secure, and then that the waterproof zips and the bleeder valve were closed. Little else would kill me as fast as my dry bag filling with water and dragging me to the bottom of the ocean.

Slowly, the rear door on the ramp of the MC-130 lowered and the fresh night air rushed into the aircraft. As the first commando in line, I waddled along, carefully navigating my giant black fins around any obstructions, to a position two steps from the right rear parachute door. I had an uninterrupted view out into the darkness.

It was a clear night. The lights of Townsville had long since disappeared over the horizon, and above the aircraft the stars stretched out forever. This was a great night for jumping. I knew from our briefings that somewhere to my right was Magnetic Island, but we were far enough away that we couldn't see it. I also knew that the closest part of the Capricornia coast was Kissing Point, a name I was told referred to the fact that tiger and hammerhead sharks mated just a few kilometres out.

I was in the follow-on force. The rest of the Commando Company had put the boats together on the beach hours ago and made their way through the darkness to the landing zone. For the first pass into the drop zone there would be twelve of us jumping in pairs, with about a 30-second gap between us. The restricting factor was the limited numbers of safety craft on the water: just six boats to pick us up, along with our chutes. Somewhere out there too was the worker boat, so designated because its role was to accept the wet parachutes from the rubber Zodiac boats.

The green light came on and I waddled further forward, to be greeted by the dispatcher. He leant down, his face a few inches from my ear. 'Go!'

I barely heard his yell over the engine noise, but the slap he gave me on the back was enough incentive. Three steps forward, and on my fourth I was met with thin air and then a rush of wind that caught my fins. My legs were ripped violently away from under me. Briefly they were thrown up and over my head, then they were slammed the other way, before the wind dragged me out into the depths of space. I hated this shit at the best of times.

'One thousand . . . and two thousand . . . and three thousand . . .' *Crack!* Then a sudden stop and I was floating. 'Thank fuck for that.'

When your parachute opens, you're met with the most beautiful sound you'll ever hear, especially on an evening when there's no wind: absolute silence. Perhaps it was the feeling of being reborn, or perhaps my senses were just on overdrive, but I loved that sound. As much as I hated heights, I'd jump every day just to hear it.

I controlled my chute and made small corrections with the wooden toggles to keep myself steady. I looked around and spotted my mate, Pat. He was only a few metres away but it wasn't a concern as he too had adjusted his chute to ride into the wind. We sailed quietly downwards, in space and time, towards the ocean below— or, as Einstein and Brian Cox would put it, as the world rose slowly to meet us.

A few seconds later I pulled my legs back out of the way and let go of the lowering line. My pack reached terminal velocity as it fell, then it hit the water with a thud. I imagined a fish tank, and how all the fish come to the surface when they sense food—then I blocked the thought. Placing my thumbs through the harness and the metal Capewell releases that secured me to the chute, I prepared to let the right side go. My feet hit the water and I pulled hard on the right D-ring, collapsing the right side of the parachute and stopping the wind from dragging me across the black water. I sunk, fast. Then resurfaced and spat out the salty water I had sampled.

I lay on my back as I went through my drills and escaped the harness. My chute was a mess, and the risers (the cords that connect the chute to the pack tray and harness) had started to wrap around my legs and back. I fought for a moment to get free, drinking some more water in the process, and then had the sudden realisation that the situation required me to stay calm and cut myself free.

I searched my jump belt for my hook knife but found the sheath empty: the small orange plastic knife had been ripped clear during the jump or the violent landing. I relaxed my body and took a deep breath, then let myself sink underwater, folding into a ball so that I could reach the dagger attached to my ankle. I tried to release it but it would not budge an inch: the risers were wrapped around the handle, binding it against my leg. I came back to the surface and the chute started to envelop my shoulders.

Pat swam over to me in the dark. 'You alright, old mate?'

'Yep, just a bit wrapped up.' I struggled again and then relaxed. I felt like a kitten with a ball of wool.

'Just relax and work your way free,' Pat replied.

I could sense him smiling at the thought of the ribbing he would give me later, in front of our section. I gave him the obvious response and continued to try to disentangle myself. If ever there was an example of why we have such a rigorous swim test for Special Forces, this was it. I was treading water one-legged, fully clothed and wrapped in a parachute.

It soon became obvious that I wouldn't be getting free on my own. 'I need a hand, mate.' Asking that—admitting defeat—was one of the hardest things I've had to do.

Pat didn't say a thing. He ducked under the water, knife in hand and went at it. I trod water with my free leg and arm. Pat swam around me for at least twenty minutes, cutting the risers here and there, and generally destroying a piece of equipment kindly provided by the Australian taxpayer.

'Where are the boats?' I asked, peering out into the blackness.

'No idea—they should've been here by now,' Pat replied, before ducking underwater again to try to release my feet. When he came to the surface again, we stopped swimming and talking and just listened. Nothing. I looked around—just sea and stars. I couldn't identify any shapes that resembled land at all. No landmarks, no lights, just a huge expanse of ocean, the gentle movement of the swell, and the Milky Way far above us.

The weight of the chute pulled me under again, and I gagged on the saltwater. It took another ten minutes of work before I escaped the chute. Finally I removed the harness and sank it, giving the harness pack a kick with my finned foot for good measure. Because of the mission profile we hadn't taken any parachute floatation devices, and so the packs were deep-sixed, straight to the bottom, a present for the edge of the Great Barrier Reef.

Pat had earned the nickname 'Admiral' for his love of boats and all things nautical. I listened while he told me how to fix the boat crews' incompetence—all manner of things had clearly gone wrong, he told me, and there were better techniques we should have been using.

We strained our ears again. I heard the MC-130 in the distance, and then its engines changed.

'Bloody hell, mate,' I said. 'We might be in the pickle here.'

The aircraft was dropping guys a long way away—it was almost inaudible. And that meant the safety boats were over there too.

An hour passed. Pat and I were great friends (he was actually my second-in-command). We had shared many experiences together already, and in future years we would have many more. In time I would become his son's godfather, and he would repay the sentiment by being the godfather of my youngest son. But for the moment we had one concern: being picked up by the boats.

I vividly remember not being scared. I was with one of my best mates in the world, and we were trained for this. If we had to, we would start slowly swimming in the direction of the mainland, which was 20 kilometres away, maybe more. Either way, we would make it.

We were dressed in camouflage uniforms, not dry suits or wetsuits. The water had been warm at first, but now my body heat was escaping. I shivered involuntarily.

Out in the darkness, someone cracked a Cyalume stick and began waving it about his head, then another. Soon there was a sea of lights, as each crew in turn snapped the safety device to attract attention. Pat and I took ours from our belts and cracked them too.

It was maybe an hour and a half after our jump, but clearly no one had been picked up. There was probably 800 metres between all of us as the current and the tide had gone to work. Our lights stretched out in a long arc, which moved up and down with the ocean.

Suddenly a black Zodiac boat, crewed by men also in black, materialised out of the dark, its twin 25-horsepower motors screaming in displeasure as they were pushed to full power. 'You guys alright?' came the call.

'Yep,' I replied, and we started to swim towards the boat.

But as fast as it had arrived, the Zodiac took off to check on another crew. I dropped the C-bomb as it disappeared into the dark.

Pat and I sat there for another fifteen minutes and finally the boat returned, full of commandos resembling drowned rats. We clambered aboard and the crew made for home. There was no point going to the worker boat: the other boat crews had all made the same decision as us and deep-sixed their parachutes.

Back at the boat ramp we were greeted with urns of soup, coffee and meat pies. If you've ever jumped out of an aircraft in the dead of night in your cotton camouflage pyjamas, bobbed around in the ocean for a few hours and then sat shivering in the bottom of a rubber boat as its hull smashed over the waves for 20 kilometres back to shore, then maybe you know just how good a meat pie, a hot shower and a sleep can be!

When I look back on this episode now, I recognise that I was in a desperate situation for a while there—and the outcome could have been much worse. Yet I was never more than slightly concerned, because I was with my best mate and we were trained to deal with the very issues that we faced.

Mateship increases your ability to cope with stressors that might otherwise be overwhelming. It's a force multiplier for your resilience. Think about it: being alone, wrapped in a parachute, bobbing around in the ocean at night, far away from land would be terrifying if you were by yourself. Throw your best mate in there with you, and now you have an adventure and an awesome story to tell twenty years later.

LESSONS

A problem shared is a problem halved. It's an old saying but it underlines the power of mateship.

When you need someone to give you confidence that your situation is not that bad and you'll get out of it eventually, a mate can be a powerful positive influence.

Mates tend to be more in tune with you than just friends so they understand and can empathise with what you're going through.

When you're about to depart on a seemingly impossible mission, the presence of a mate makes the journey less daunting.

5

BE PREPARED—AND BE ADAPTABLE

'In pursuit of knowledge, every day something is acquired;
In pursuit of wisdom, every day something is dropped.'

Lao Tzu, Chinese philosopher, c. 6th century BC

We never stop learning, but sometimes the familiarity of our social setting, our work environment or the day-to-day challenges we face can affect our ability to respond to change. In my experience, the most successful people are those who can let go of a skill or concept in order to operate better in a new environment. Let me give you a couple of examples.

I'm an avid packer. I take joy out of lining things up, placing them in order and checking items off lists to make sure everything is ready to go. But one packing experience I remember very well was one I didn't enjoy.

It was a cold autumn day at Holsworthy Barracks, in south-west Sydney, in 1997. The rain tapped gently against my window as I cast an eye over my single bed. It was covered in equipment, all items either in a stuff sack, rolled up and held together with elastic bands or in purpose-designed cases. Nearly everything had Velcro on it some-where. Most of the items were black or green or had been painted camouflage.

There was a summer sleeping bag, a winter sleeping bag, a bivvy bag, a hoochie shelter, two torches (because one is none), spare batteries, socks, two sets of boots, two knives, a solid fuel hexamine stove (Hexi) made out of a cut-down canteen, plastic collapsible water bladders, a spork and a FRED. (The latter is a combination can opener and miniature spoon; the acronym stands for Field Ration Eating Device, but soldiers know it as a Fucking Ridiculous Eating Device). On the floor was a suitcase, and next to it an ALICE (All-purpose Lightweight Individual Carrying Equipment) pack and my chest webbing.

I checked the items for a second time, just to make sure I hadn't missed anything, then slowly placed them in my pack. I picked up the joining instruction I'd been issued and looked over the list again: nowhere did it say pack and webbing. There were no field items at all, actually, and yet I'd been told I would be heading into the field a few days after I arrived at the Commando Training Centre for the Royal Marines, at Exmouth, in the United Kingdom.

I put my pack and webbing back in the bottom of my wardrobe, and then began packing a suitcase with my civilian clothes. As I looked at the small case sitting on the floor, I realised I was about to venture more than halfway around the world with little equipment and just a few clothes, and yet within a week I'd be out field-training young marines. I shuddered at the thought of using unfamiliar field equipment.

I had spent years getting my gear just right. My hoochie, for example, had rubber straps with personally engineered loops so that I could tie it on any tree and at any angle. I had perfected its use both in dense jungle and in open country, where the large-trunked gum trees are notoriously hard to tie off on. I had painted it too, one side for the jungle and the other for the desert.

Most of the other things I owned had also been through my own rigorous research and development phase. I owned half of the best gear that Platatac had ever designed, and I cringed when other guys would make fun of new guys with 'all the gear and no idea': deep down, I knew I was probably also compensating for a lack of knowledge about some things, covering it by the purchase of the latest bit of equipment.

I landed in England a few days later. It was summer, and I took to my surroundings easily. Not long after I arrived, I was introduced to the Deer Leap, a quiet pub that overlooked the Exe Estuary, where I sampled the warm ale and relaxed in the English version of the sun. The next day I was taken on a tour around the Royal Marines' base, where I would be working as a Corporal Instructor over the coming months, and I was introduced to my training platoon. Then it was off to the quartermaster's store to pick up my new equipment.

It was all very different from what I was used to. The pack was huge and modular, the equipment clunky, and everything seemed to be box-shaped. Combat 95, they called it, a project that had been in the works for a few years and only just now was delivering new equipment to the Marines. Their version of a personal shelter was massive and came with telescopic poles, because there were no trees on Dartmoor; putting it up required a completely different skill to any I had been taught.

Even my basic tools of trade weren't the same. The Silva compass I had brought from home didn't work because it was the Southern Hemisphere version. The needle pointed in the opposite direction— which I would have anticipated, had I paid more attention on the reconnaissance course I'd done a few years earlier.

This experience was my first lesson about the danger of clinging to the things we know and not keeping an open mind about what we actually need. Karl E. Weick gave a keynote address in 1996 called 'Drop Your Tools', which really resonated with me. '[H]uman potential is realized as much by what we drop, as what we acquire,' Weick commented. He uses the example of American firefighters who had perished while retreating from a wildfire. They tried to hang onto their power saws, axes and backpacks; if they'd dropped them, they would likely have been able to get to safety. The lesson was that they hadn't adapted to the challenge of their current setting.

In my case, the 'tools' were the equipment that I'd spent years using. Applying what I'd learnt in my training in the Australian military had always worked for me, and I was arguably at the top of my game as a young corporal. But now I was in a foreign land, literally. I had to learn new skills, and adapt my existing skills for different operating conditions, all while trying to teach young Royal Marines the art of soldiering.

The experience taught me a vital lesson, one that would see me become more successful in some very difficult circumstances in the future. The key takeaway was to learn to adapt, and adapt fast, to new skills or techniques. I needed to dump my old tools, and replace them with new ones that were appropriate in this new operating environment. Weick argues that 'people may refuse to drop their tools because of problems with hearing, trust, control, physical well-being, and calculation'. For almost all these reasons, my instinct was to try to cling to what I knew. But I was forced to let go and accept that I couldn't operate as effectively in this new setting. It was a powerful lesson.

———

More than thirteen years later, I witnessed some other young and very smart Australian commandos have a similar epiphany. We were travelling along a dirt track about 40 kilometres south-south-east of Tarin Kowt, Afghanistan, on the third day of a disrupt operation. The aim was to broadcast to the local people that we were operating in the area.

This was easily done: we had a Mercedes Unimog mothership carrying backup supplies and ammunition, four-wheel and six-wheel motorbikes for our snipers and recon to conduct pathfinding and route selection, and eleven Bushmaster Protected Mobility Vehicles

(PMVs) all kicking up dust. Think the Spanish Armada but on land, and with a giant Australian flag being flown on the lead vehicle.

The idea was that the enemy would talk about us, and maybe shoot at us. The SASR troop we were partnered with would then conduct helicopter-targeting operations off the back of the interest that we created. It wasn't rocket science—in fact, we referred to it as a 'tethered goat operation'. We were bait.

On this morning, we were moving towards a village. I had dismounted my snipers a few hours before, and they had gone on foot into the hills to conduct a rolling overwatch of our convoy. They had a simple mission: engage anyone out there who was manoeuvring with hostile intent. I trusted my people implicitly to make the right choice about who was hostile and who was not. 'If you have to ask me to shoot, then you don't have permission,' I'd told them. They had my permission to engage if the threat met all the conditions on the Red Card for Orders for Opening Fire. It was that simple.

They had departed without a word of complaint. The payoff for trekking into the steep hills in the middle of the hot day was that they were left to do what snipers are paid to do: hunt the enemy. The snipers were at times as far as 10 kilometres in front of the main body, and at times the two teams were 2 kilometres apart. We had procedures in place if they got bumped. They could call in fire when they were in range of our platoon mortars, as well as artillery and Fast Air (close air support, or CAS, provided by fixed-wing ground attack jet aircraft) when beyond it. With the snipers deep in the hills, we started to proceed forward.

The biggest risk to my platoon was the threat of an improvised explosive device (IED) strike. Our engineers were the unsung heroes of the task group. Out there in front, in the stifling heat and the dust, they used metal detectors and detection dogs to unearth all manner of sneaky things that go bang. And our engineers were on the ball: they managed to find an entirely wooden pressure plate and assembly.

Obviously, the bad guys had clued on that we would find their IEDs with our minelabs (metal detectors), but there were still a few small metal components they needed to use, such as copper wiring and battery packs.

Our guys were so switched on, or just plain mistrustful, that they picked up the faintest sound from the copper wiring. On excavation, they found that the pressure plate, battery pack and diesel fuel and fertiliser had been distributed as far away from each other as possible, to lower the chance of being detected. They hadn't counted on us having engineers who could find wood with a metal detector. The engineer who detected it was a humble professional, and I'm positive that his actions saved a lot of people that day.

Given that the snipers were gone for the day, I moved their vehicle up front and we dropped the engineers' vehicle behind it. The sniper vehicle just had one person on board, the Royal Australian Armoured Corp (RAAC) driver, Trooper Bailey. The engineers cleared the road all the way to the night vehicle harbour. Trooper Bailey's vehicle followed, and all the other drivers judiciously kept in the tracks of the lead vehicle.

We arrived at our destination a few hours before last light, and radioed the snipers to make their way to us. We kept our guns and mortars trained on the hills in the distance, ready to provide them with fire support once they were in range.

The drivers slowly manoeuvred their vehicles into the harbour and lined them up to sit at specific points on an imaginary clock face, a technique that allowed us to achieve all-round defence with our platoon weapons. Then Bails shifted his Bushmaster a few feet to get a better position—and BOOM!

I watched from the front seat of my vehicle as the Bushmaster was picked up and spun around on its axles. The front wheel flying past my windscreen, and equipment was cast into the heavens. A fire started on the side of the vehicle and then spread around the car.

We had a set of procedures to follow in such an event, and we went about our business calmly. Platoon Sergeant Paul Cale managed the initial response. He lost his shit for a few minutes while getting the response underway, then he settled into business as usual as he went through the drills. The rest of the platoon conducted initial sweeps of their areas to make sure there was no more IEDs. Bailey was retrieved from the vehicle, shaken but not stirred, and we let the Bushmaster burn to the ground.

The only thing we really worried about was grabbing the 84-millimetre mortar and ammunition. The snipers had most of their expensive weapons and optics with them, and some of their personal weapons (M4s) were also retrieved. Their expensive and personal packs were all lost in the fire, though.

The snipers returned to the platoon location, guided by the plume of smoke, and were met by the sight of a smouldering carcass of a vehicle. If they lost their shit, I never saw it. The platoon swapped equipment around to make sure there was an even distribution across a few Bushmasters and we gave the snipers a now empty vehicle. We also scrounged what spare equipment we had and gave that to them too. I called in an aerial resupply over the next few days and we supplemented their equipment with things that the quarter-master store had at its disposal. We couldn't replace the snipers' personal equipment—much of which they had acquired over years in their trade—but they had enough to make do.

The lads were learning the same lesson I had been given while at the Royal Marines' training centre years before. The equipment snipers use is an extension of their professionalism, but it's their knowledge that makes them a sniper. They could do the job with less than optimal gear.

As if to reinforce this lesson, the same thing happened again a few days later: Trooper Bailey gained the nickname 'Bang Bang', and the snipers had to get some more fresh kit. I know these lessons helped shape them into the successful soldiers and men they would become.

Being adaptable isn't just about your tools of the trade. It applies to every aspect of your life. It is a strength you can draw upon. It's so important to find ways to deal with change and uncertainty—by developing resilience and a positive mindset, for instance. The words of Karl Weick still resonate with me: 'If you drop tools, then ideas have more free play. Just think of the maxim that when you have a hammer, the entire world turns into things that need to be nailed. Take that one step further. If you drop your hammer, then the world is no longer a world of mere nails.'

LESSONS

You are the asset, not the tool. Don't get married to your equipment.

Your knowledge and experience are infinitely expandable. Your tools are not.

The sense of security you feel in becoming expert in the use of tools can obstruct your true understanding. Imagine the day these tools are removed. This is when you are either exposed or emboldened. Choose emboldened.

Drop comfort in the pursuit of wisdom.

Be at a standard of professionalism where you can get the job done with the bare minimum. Anything more is a one-percenter, at best.

6

RESET YOUR FRAME OF REFERENCE

'Staying positive does not mean that things will
turn out okay, rather it is knowing that you will be
okay no matter how things turned out.'

A frame of reference is essential to persevering through adversity. What's not often talked about, though, is that it is a perishable mindset, so you need to constantly experience or remember those times when you've done it tougher and come through, to keep your faith in yourself at the front of your mind. One way to do this is through meditation.

There's a simple beauty to meditation. I've lots of great friends who rave about its benefits. One of these mates is TV star Daniel MacPherson, who religiously uses the *Headspace* app. This guy is super grounded, and he projects joy and positivity into the world. I truly believe a big reason he's as successful as he is is because of his ability to focus due to meditation. Another friend who meditates daily is Ian Prior, the captain of the Western Force rugby union side. He's also an inspiration. Although not as big as the other guys on his team, or arguably as genetically gifted, he's the hardest worker in any room and chases his goals like a man possessed. This is attributable to the time he spends thinking deeply and meditating.

So it may come as a surprise when I tell you that I don't meditate. That's not to say I don't understand its benefits, because I do. What I do is something different, though. I sit and think deeply about my frames of reference, and occasionally I commit myself to reset-ting them.

A frame of reference is an event or situation that you have experienced before. It's an event where you've endured, perhaps suffered, and usually prevailed. It can also be a powerful positive memory of something great, something that you can draw strength from, or something that in your darkest hour you can look back on and think, 'Remember when I did this thing that was harder than this?' It's my strong belief that if you have a frame of reference that's worse or more difficult than your current situation, then it's easier to tell yourself, 'Hey, this isn't so bad.' That's the starting point. My most powerful frame of reference came when, as a young soldier in an infantry battalion, I had an experience that stayed with me forever.

In 1994 I went to the Jungle Warfare Training Centre in Far North Queensland again, but this time as a lance corporal. My section commander was sick and so we got a new one in, Stephen McCaig. He was a great soldier and well liked across the unit, although I thought he was a bit of a bully. As it turned out, he wasn't—he was just a hard taskmaster, and as the second-in-charge I bore the brunt of his demands. There's a big difference between being a bully and being a hard boss, as I would work out in the years to come. Anyway, I did my job and he did his, and we ran the section together. We didn't know each other terribly well, but that didn't matter—we just got on and did what we were there for.

We'd been in the rain and the thick, dark jungle for two weeks. At the end of the exercise, there was one activity left to do: a stretcher carry from the famous Earls Court back to the start of the obstacle course—12 kilometres in total. What's more, it would be a race against the other sections in the company.

We started with a section of nine men, but pretty soon, due to injuries—perceived or real, I couldn't be sure—we were down to seven. This meant that we had four men to carry the stretcher and two spares. (One guy had to be lying on the stretcher.) Our two spare guys were proving less and less effective, and soon the swap-outs on the stretcher became less frequent. It was raining steadily, our uniforms were chafing us and we hadn't eaten properly in two weeks. We also had to carry our packs and rifles, and put up with the directing staff shadowing us and yelling out all sorts of colourful and negative encouragement. Our feet were blistered, and our skin was itchy from prickly heat. We had no energy and were all pretty short with each other.

It wasn't long before Stephen and I stopped swapping out from stretcher-carrying duties. We were leading by example and forcing the pace. Some men become silent under adversity, and venture into a place in their minds where they can still continue. We call this being 'in the hurt locker'. I don't do that. On the contrary, I don't shut up. I push and motivate, and usually I'm able to help people lift and give their best. Stephen was like me, so we relentlessly encouraged and coerced our section to move the stretcher forward.

On and on we went until we got to the obstacle course, and that's where the quiet guys suddenly became vocal. They were excited at the prospect of getting to the start of the end, as they knew it would all be over soon. This enraged me.

We finished the obstacle course, and I shared a moment with Stephen. A quiet look of admiration for each other formed the basis of a lifelong friendship. Then we turned our attention to the guys who hadn't put in the effort. My previous hardest frame of reference had been reset.

———

My life is now a series of frames of reference, memories that have helped me make sense of a situation, decide on a course of action, or shape a solution to a problem. These frames of reference have shaped my personality and ultimately helped me develop and maintain my resilience.

- As a child, the warmth of the shower after football on a cold winter's day. This is my first frame of reference, and it's a gentle one. The sense of reward here is evident.
- The comfort of flannel sheets, the kiss goodnight of Grandma and the tick of a vintage clock. For me as an eight-year-old, this was bliss. It's a frame of reference that helps me appreciate the things in life that protect us.
- The smell of Gillette lemon shaving cream, the frantic need to shave in under five minutes, and the flinch of being yelled at to 'clear the ablutions and stand by your bed'. My Kapooka frame of reference built my need to always have a sense of urgency.
- The smell of rain on hot bitumen, freshly cut grass and lamb chops on the barbecue. This frame of reference drew me back to Adelaide every year for my annual leave, Christmas after Christmas.
- The sounds of cockatoos at dawn, the cool breeze that will ultimately give way to sweltering heat, and the sound of the Salvation Army truck horn promising coffee and Nice biscuits. Something good always happens; just give it time.
- The sound of rolling thunder. The first drops of water on an iron roof. Rain on the brim of a bush hat, and then on my face. Finally, the sodden feeling of a wet camouflage uniform, and knowing that I can survive this for days, weeks, indefinitely.
- The unbearable pain in my chest and legs as we ran up Trigg Point, on the Perth coastline. The effort is gruelling as the platoon commander turns us around and has us running to the top again, and again, and again. A frame of reference is set, a reminder that all pain will end at some point. Now I'm running to the bottom, pleading in my own mind that we do it again as

if it's the most important thing in the world. 'Please, let's do it again, please, boss, please . . .' The frame of reference: *I won't be fooled by you again, sir. I'd rather die than show you I don't want to run up here.*

During the year I took to write this book, I devoted myself to mentoring leaders all over the country. Yet I felt like I was weakening: my body and mind needed a challenge. My frames of reference were not as potent as they had been. They were fading.

I signed up for an Olympic triathlon in Dubai. If I trained hard, I knew I'd be competitive—but it would also rule my life. So I trained enough to be confident of finishing, and that was all. I did just one swim prior to the race, a 1.5-kilometre trial in the pool. It was hard, physically and mentally, but I survived. What I didn't realise was that I'd had one of those great days when you just feel unstoppable. I had breezed through the swim—it was easy.

A few weeks later, I was on the starting line looking out to the Arabian Sea. The starter's horn went off and I walked into the water and began to swim. It was torture. The chop was up, it was windy, and I couldn't settle into the stroke and took in lots of water. It was also a two-lap circuit, which is hard mentally at the best of times.

I was maintaining my effort okay when someone behind me grabbed my ankle and pulled me back to get ahead. I lost my mind, my adrenaline spiked and I wanted revenge. I was starting to waste energy, I realised, so I had to control my emotions. When finally I exited the water, it was with huge relief. I felt like shit: I was trying to just stay upright and not throw up.

The cycle leg was equally tough, windy and hot. I struggled to maintain my race plan. *The run is where the magic is going to happen,* I decided. *This is frame of reference territory.*

I started out at a pace of just under 4:15 minutes per kilometre. But I've been around long enough to know how to finish a

10-kilometre run at the end of an Olympic-distance triathlon, and it's not by setting a new PB, so I slowed my pace, choosing 5:45 as my speed. Six kilometres in, with the temperature at 38 degrees plus and the hot wind swirling, I was in the pain cave and establishing a new frame of reference.

I began drawing on old memories of ambushes, long insertions under huge loads over rocky and mountainous terrain, night swims when I'd dragged waterproof packs through tumultuous surf zones, Klepper kayak insertions that lasted from sundown to sunrise, skiing in a whiteout blizzard in subzero temperatures, standing on the airfield in Tarin Kowt with a hundred other commandos as the bodies of our mates were slowly driven past in coffins . . . All these memories flooded back to me, and then finally it happened:

'One more step . . . One more step . . . One more step . . .'

BOOM! There it was. This was a mantra that tied all of my frames of reference together.

Most successful Special Forces guys I know have fallen back on this technique at one time or another. It becomes hypnotic. It is my meditation. It takes a long time to get to the euphoric point where the pain disappears, or at the very least becomes manageable, but it does happen.

Me: 'I can't do this.'

Coach (also me): 'Not with that attitude, you can't.'

Me: 'Okay, well, I've done harder in the past.'

Coach: 'Show me.'

One more step.

———

On the first day of 2020, I went for a run. Not because I wanted to, but out of necessity. I had consumed a few too many drinks the night before and had wisely left the car at the venue. As you can imagine, the run wasn't particularly easy; I was hungover, it was breezy, there were a few inclines along the 10-kilometre route that make the profile of this run a challenge at the best of times and the temperature was already creeping into the mid-30s. I struggled through the run, retrieved the car and proceeded to refuel and recover.

Later that day I saw that my friend Rob, who is based in the UAE, had posted a challenge on his Instagram page, encouraging his followers to run 10 kilometres a day for ten days. I considered the challenge: 'Well, I've already run the first ten kilometres, I may as well run another nine. It can't be that hard, right?'

HOW WRONG I WAS.

What followed was an interesting experiment not only in fitness but in resetting my frames of reference as well. During the process I learnt much about self-motivation (or lack thereof), consistency, priorities, mental toughness, recovery and accountability. Here are the eight things I have taken away from running 10 kilometres a day for ten days that will help me make sense of future challenges.

Commit. Committing to something on social media creates a high level of accountability. I guess this is a no brainer but for those of you who may not see the benefit of this, think about how a public commitment can be a motivational tool. By telling my community/tribe that I was committing I was also allowing them to hold me accountable for completing the challenge.

Schedule. When you commit to something and then schedule time to get it done it reinforces the importance of that commitment. I've said it 1000 times before, but 'show me a person's schedule and I'll show you their priorities'. I'm a busy guy. Much of my activity is self-driven. I have to schedule things to manage competing projects and priorities. In many cases if it's not scheduled, it's just not getting done. I scheduled time from 5.45 am to 7.45 am every day to get the run and other associated tasks completed. If it's important you will schedule it. If it's in the schedule, then it's a priority and you'll get it done. Time is the cost and time is your most valuable commodity. You can't buy more . . . and the clock is ticking.

Set yourself up for success. If you have committed to something and then scheduled it, the rest of your day starts to support that commitment. The runs took me, on average, 55 minutes, give or take five minutes either side. I didn't just roll out of bed and start running, though. I needed to organise my morning routine to support the schedule. This involved laying out my running gear the night before, taking a quick drive to an area I like to run around, writing in my gratitude journal and having a black coffee—setting myself up physically and emotionally to tackle the run. Then there was the after-run Instagram post, data check-in and connection with those supporting me. Remember, it's not about proving your doubters wrong—it's about proving your supporters right! As it is in life.

Create the right habits. Running 10 kilometres a day is about recovery as much as the actual running. This should have been pretty easy for me given I ran all through high school and the Army loves to make you run; I've got the volume in the legs for this challenge. But honestly, I did find it tough. As I immersed myself deeper in the challenge, I realised that I needed the right habits to recover properly. This involved foam rolling and stretching, something I had never really done before. I hadn't seen the benefit; being sore was just a part of training for me. There was also the requirement to hydrate properly during the day and at night, so as not to tank during the run. I needed to build these habits throughout the day.

See mental toughness as an opportunity. Mental toughness and the endurance needed to complete the runs were of equal importance. Some days I struggled to put one foot in front of the other. On other days the accumulation of the distance felt like it was taking its toll and I had to check my internal negative dialogue. At one point I let my ego get the better of me and hung onto the pace of a person who overtook me. This proved disastrous on the return leg. I only just completed the run. I called on existing frames of reference to just get to the starting line, to put one foot in front of the other, to trust the process and to maintain a positive outlook for the duration of the 10 kilometres. A metaphor for life.

Same bat time, same bat channel. I don't usually like setting patterns—call it a learnt survival instinct. However, running the same track each day at the same time was a grounding experience. I got to experience the sunrise, the changes in the weather, people and even the changes in the light. It's great for perspective on the ever-changing experience that is life. Being outdoors at the start of every day gave me a sense of grounding.

Wins lead to winning. Running 10 kilometres a day for ten days was about the little wins for the big win. Waking in the morning is a great start to the day, the first win. After that I'd reward myself with an espresso at my favourite café that's close to the start line. Getting to the start line was the next win. Then there was the first step into my run, making it up the little hill, catching up to the person in front, maintaining my pace for another kilometre. All of these are little wins. On getting to the 5-kilometre mark I would reward myself by taking off my t-shirt. Another win.

Now what? I finished the ten-day challenge and felt the sense of achievement on completing the mission. But when I woke up the next day something was missing. I slept through my normal wake up time. My sense of purpose wasn't really there. I didn't fill out my gratitude journal, nor did I get my morning coffee. Instead of discipline and accountability there was an emptiness. It wasn't my body that wanted to run, it was my mind.

Running 10 kilometres for ten days; it's not really that big a deal. However, I found it a great reset of my commitment, consistency, discipline and mental toughness, too. New frames of reference, if you will.

LESSONS

All hardship eventually ends. You can always take one more step and be closer to the comfort and familiarity that makes you feel safe.

Resetting your frame of reference and reminding yourself that you've come through tougher situations in the past means you can challenge yourself to get out of your comfort zone and achieve things you never thought possible.

Doing something hard just once doesn't cut it. Don't fall into the trap of comfort years after achieving something great.

Continually challenge yourself. Not all challenges are physical, and nor should they be. If you're a physical monster, challenge yourself academically—and vice versa.

The best part of a challenging experience comes when it's over!

Remember, you are your most important mission.

7

TREAT BOREDOM AS AN OPPORTUNITY

'A generation that cannot endure boredom will be a
generation of little men . . . in whom every vital impulse
slowly withers as though they were cut flowers in a vase.'

Bertrand Russell

I experienced countless hours of boredom in my Army life. Sometimes it was so arduous that I contemplated discharge. However,
somewhere along the way I learnt that being bored can be advan-
tageous. Boredom can in fact be a powerful tool that sparks creativity,
wonderment and inspiration. It can help us develop amazing ideas
and even solve some of the world's, and our own, deepest problems.

It might sound strange, but some of my most vivid memories
of my time in the Army and Special Forces are of being on sentry
duty (or piquet, as we called it). I did such incredible things, so
why is it that I can remember, in amazing detail, benign events like
lying on sodden earth in a rain-swept jungle while training in Far
North Queensland, or the instant the wind changed from hot to cold
while I was sitting on top of an armoured vehicle in Somalia. Only
moments before, I had been bored out of my mind, just staring out
into the desert.

I remember the terror I felt at night in Afghanistan, shivering up
on a rocky escarpment while my men slept in a small ravine behind
me. I peered out into the darkness searching for an enemy who knew
only too well how to blend into the rocks. Far down in the valley
below, artillery and fast jets hammered an enemy position, while the

US Special Forces escaped an ambush that had been set for them. A drone circled overhead, silent in the darkness. I watched it all unfold, and when it had finished I looked up to the stars and my thoughts drifted to the time at school when I'd fought with a bigger kid who had my measure.

Every soldier has had to pull a sentry duty at some time in their career, either alone or with someone else. You sit there and listen and watch for the enemy while the rest of your team sleeps or carries out work behind you, usually out of earshot. The effort of staying awake can be exhausting; filling our every waking moment with stimulus, as most of us do these days, is really a very new thing. Some sentry duties I've done were just 25 minutes, others in excess of three hours, but the ones I remember most vividly are solo duties by night, in the era before we had night-vision goggles. I didn't want them to end.

Here's the thing. When you're sitting there bored, you slowly become one with the environment. You tune into your surroundings, become a silent voyeur of everything that's going on around you. The flora, the fauna, the weather—all these things become existential, in that their existence explains itself to you.

As a young soldier, I had one sentry duty somewhere in the high range training area in Queensland. I was alone, sitting in the heat of the day on a rock, trying not to fall asleep, but my eyelids had other ideas. The exercise wasn't contested, so I knew there was no enemy out there—and it's really hard to stay motivated when there's no enemy. I was daydreaming about all manner of things: girls, motorbikes, girls, triathlon, girls, and my future—normal soldier stuff—when I felt a weight on my knees.

Slowly, I looked down—and saw a king brown snake casually sliding across my outstretched legs. He looked up at me, and then back in the direction he was going. It was like waiting for a giant cargo train to pass: the carriages just kept on coming, and I estimated that it was almost 3 metres in length. I was surprised at how calm

I was. There was no time for 'flight or fight', so the adrenaline never kicked in. He slid away slowly, in the direction of my platoon a few hundred metres away.

I continued my sentry duty, contemplating nature and the profound experience I'd just had with this reptile, which could have easily ended my life. That was until I heard screams below me, and saw people running everywhere. Perhaps my platoon had just seen a snake . . .

I didn't know it back then, but I was actually building a skill: I was learning to be bored. I was discovering the power of mindfulness—of keeping your attention in the moment—which is a building block of emotional intelligence, and perhaps even a precursor to enlightenment. Mindfulness is the art of projecting your thoughts and imagining outcomes, training your brain to make informed decisions, and mentally exploring plans to discover their second- and third-order effects. In boredom I had discovered a form of meditation that allowed me to develop my subconscious along with my conscious mind.

And when I say I discovered the power of boredom, what I really mean is I stumbled upon it. Let's face it, thinkers have done this for millennia. Philosophers, scientists, mathematicians, psychologists, writers and others have sat and been bored, giving their minds the space to think deeply about things.

Having spent all that time on the piquet, I can now just sit mindfully with little effort. The beautiful thing is that it's not a difficult skill to learn. You just need to let yourself be bored occasionally. You can train yourself to work through it, and not need the constant stimulation of society or distraction. If you give yourself the space to try, you can become someone who thinks deeply, reflects, ponders and imagines things.

Ideally, find somewhere in nature, somewhere quiet and hidden away. Leave your distractions at home. Your mind needs to be observant of the benign things surrounding you. Just look around.

Be observant. Ask yourself questions about things. If you see an ant, think about how fast it's moving, relative to its size. The patterns in the leaves and the tree bark—why are they like that? Why do clouds look like they do, and how do they form? Observe everything and talk to yourself in your mind.

Then, half an hour later, unpack an idea. (You can use your watch; trust me, soldiers on piquet check their watches every couple of minutes too.) Contemplate something deeper. Think about religion, creation, your life, your future or your past—just let your thoughts wander. Come up with some hypothesis that explains what you've been thinking about, or an action plan to implement.

You can train your mind in this way in your daily life, too. If you can't remember something—a singer's name, a book title, anything really—don't immediately reach for Google. Allow your mind to ponder the matter, and come back to it later. You knew the answer before, so it's still in there! Allowing your mind to work the question out itself will bolster its abilities for the future.

If you do this regularly, you'll find that the decisions you make will be better informed, you'll solve problems naturally rather than react to issues, and in this way you'll realise more of your own potential. All this comes from being comfortable with being bored.

LESSONS

Don't look at being bored as time you've lost—it's actually time gained. Having this time to yourself can be a form of meditation that brings great benefits.

Being bored allows you to tune into your environment. Appreciate the sights, sounds, tastes, smells and feelings around you. For me, this is the perfect time to think.

Allow your mind to come up with whatever random thoughts and ideas it wants: future plans, jobs that need doing, concepts to explore, reminiscences about good times.

Whenever and wherever you find the time and space for mindful boredom, don't avoid it or waste it. Embrace it as an opportunity for creativity and growth.

8

EMBRACE THE SUCK

'The most potent tool in maintaining the status
quo is our belief that change is impossible.'

Russell Brand

In 1997 I learnt that I would be part of the first group on a new
commando training course. Immediately I knew that I was going to
struggle with physical and mental toughness. For the second time in
my career, I made a deliberate decision to become tougher, physically
and mentally. I had three months to do it.

By this time I had been in the Army for six years, so I had some
solid frames of reference to fall back on. Still, I needed to understand
how to tie it all together. So I resolved that toughness was a skill and
it could be trained.

The world can be a very harsh place, and being tough can be an
advantage. In many settings, how tough you are can be the difference
between excelling or failing. In some professions, it can even be the
difference between living or dying. I've met a lot of tough people, and
quite a few who thought they were tough. I've also seen how being
gentle can be misconstrued as weak—and this isn't always the case.

When I set myself the challenge of increasing my toughness, the
first thing I recognised was that context was important: exactly what
was it I wanted to become tougher for? I also had the suspicion that if
I could become physically fitter, that would extend my baseline abilities, giving me an extra buffer before I'd need to draw on my mental

toughness. I embarked on hard training sessions, going to the edge of my physical ability and then pushing myself past the point of failure.

I also learnt that resilience—how quickly you bounce back from a setback or hardship—is vital. Sleep, diet and mental fitness all play a part.

———

What is toughness? For me, it isn't a physical attribute, but rather a mental one that kicks in once your physical boundaries have been reached. Strength is a physical attribute, but being strong doesn't mean you're tough. It just means that you can lift more weight or transfer more power around than the next person. Being physically strong can certainly help with being tough, but I've seen plenty of strong people who were absolute snowflakes when the heat was turned up. Strong isn't tough. Not even close.

Toughness has been studied and celebrated for millennia. Being able to absorb physical as well as mental punishment in a particular context is the basis of toughness. Toughness comes from having a certain mental disposition, a mindset that is ready to take the burden once the body starts failing.

Some people like to use 'toughness' and 'resilience' interchangeably, but toughness is not resilience. I don't go for pretty words. Resilience occurs once toughness is either depleted or an event has concluded. Toughness is during the fact.

I think of it in terms of fuel tanks. I have four, and they decrease in size as they are used. Fitness is my main tank; once it's depleted, my character tank kicks in. Character is my reserve tank, if you like: the light is on but I've still got a fair bit left. Once character has been depleted, I fall back on my anger tank. Last but not least is rage. This one only lasts a few seconds, and it works great in fights as a last-ditch effort.

So how does someone go about getting tough? Well, toughness is gained in a few different ways. It's important to understand the context—what's the reason you are trying to become tough? It's similar to being fit—fit for what? For which sport? In this sense, toughness is context-specific. Tough for what?

Let's say you want to be tougher when it comes to dealing with your own personality, or in your interactions with others at work. The approach for building this type of toughness will be very different from that of someone who is intending to summit Mount Everest. Building toughness so you can complete an ironman race is different to developing the toughness you need to survive in the bush alone. Context matters, although it is true that there's some carry-over from one to the next. It's also true that a degree of toughness can be gained from immersion in a situation. Yet it still takes specific preparation to excel at being tough in a particular context, so there's lots to be gained from working on your context-specific requirements.

The following are the key areas that I would work on to build toughness. I'm going to use the context of leadership in combat, but you can easily apply these concepts to other arenas, such as work, sports or even relationships.

Being physically fit is a great starting point for toughness. Being strong, flexible and agile means that you are less impacted when you need to use your body to complete tasks. This helps to protect your mind, freeing it up to continue doing what it needs to do. Physical strength and fitness come from a mixture of adaptation to stressors and then recovery, as well as nutrition and rest. The resulting physical growth can be used to support your mental toughness.

Learning how to get yourself into the 'growth zone', or the point where fitness occurs, is also great mental conditioning. It's not easy to do and it hurts—you have to push yourself either to physical failure (when participating in body-building type workouts) or complete multiple sets of a specific effort.

For instance, when conducting metabolic or conditioning work-outs, make your last set the same as your first. There's actual science in this. Elite coaches and athletes employ a 10 per cent rule during interval training. Your first effort and every effort throughout shouldn't vary by more than 10 per cent. Discipline and consistency are the keys to success. Don't do one hard session per week, in among five suboptimal efforts—it's all about cutting out the peaks and troughs, and raising your baseline capability.

The hardest physical training I've ever done is 'brick' training. This refers to riding hard and then jumping off the bike straight into a run, then repeating that a few times to adapt to the stress. (There's something to be said for triathletes—to excel in that sport you have to build a certain type of toughness.) Quite often, I learnt, the pain you feel (both physical and emotional) is temporary: it hurts initially, but if you ride out the discomfort for a while then the pain subsides—usually a new pain takes its place! Seriously, it sucks, but in a good way.

Training myself in this type of toughness translated to other areas of my life. When I was the leader of a Special Forces platoon, I created a physical training program that would mimic some of the physical requirements that would be asked of me in combat. I'd do a pack march for 5 kilometres, carrying heavy weights, and then do a webbing run as hard as I could for 400 metres, taking myself to physical exhaustion. I'd then do maximum push-ups in two minutes, followed by maximum burpees in two minutes. Then I'd finish the workout with another pack march of 5 kilometres. This was making me physically fitter, and at the same time I was working on my mental toughness.

Being able to hold a high heart rate while under load is an unwritten requirement for a Special Forces operator, and that ability can only be got through training. Being physically fit helps, but it's not a natural type of fitness—you can't get it from going for 5-kilometre or

10-kilometre runs every other day. In Afghanistan, there were things I had to do that were well above my physical preparation or ability, but my mental toughness got me through, and a big part of that was my ability to sustain a high heart rate while under load, and then holding on until the work had finished. If I hadn't been physically fit, I wouldn't have been able to withstand long periods of adversity.

I've used environmental conditioning to build toughness too. I'd go for long runs in the winter rain. I've also ridden 50 kilometres around Al Qudra, Dubai, in the middle of a sandstorm on a 50-degree summer day—the whole point was to train my body to maintain effort in high temperatures. I go swimming when the waves are crashing around due to squalls off shore, and I've been skiing in the back country in a blizzard. I hate the idea of humans escaping the forces of nature, huddling inside like timid souls. For me, that's not living.

Environmental training is critical to toughness. As I see it, not being able to withstand the forces of nature is detrimental to the human condition. Moreover, learning to think clearly while exposed to harsh environments is crucial: the ability to compartmentalise the effects of the weather and continue making sound decisions is an incredible skill. Being cold, wet and hungry and still being able to make good decisions takes practice, and you can't practise it properly unless you experience a certain level of discomfort.

I'm not advocating that you put yourself in harm's way. You definitely shouldn't bite off more than you can chew, but you do need to stretch yourself and experience the negative impacts that the environment can have on you.

———

Let me tell you a story about a 5-kilometre run I did one afternoon in Perth. This distance is an underrated one: many people think it's easy, but its power to transform a person's fitness and heal a person's soul is great. In my experience, it's actually a complex challenge.

I started from the car park at City Beach. It was around 34 degrees and I was cruising along. My watch indicated the end of the first kilometre: I was tracking at 5:23 per kilometre pace, with a heart rate of about 120 beats per minute. The next 500 metres felt even easier, and I decided I had a couple of choices to make: take the free speed now while the going was easy, or hold something in reserve for the inevitable hard patches ahead. I decided on the latter and held back my pace.

Sometimes in life we think we're holding back, but we're not. We measure ourselves against the wrong metrics. I was thinking about how I felt, my other performances and my perceived effort. In fact, I rolled through the 2-kilometre mark in 5:00 per kilometre, with an average heart rate of 168 beats per minute. This is well within my comfort zone, but I wasn't looking at the whole picture: I figured I was just feeling really strong that day, so I kept motoring, increasing my pace and ignoring the data.

It didn't occur to me that I wasn't feeling hot, which was an indication that there was a breeze behind me. I did know I was on a slight decline, but even so that wouldn't have increased my pace by that much. I was loving this.

Then, I hit the 2.5-kilometre mark and turned around. The wind from Fremantle was immediately evident, as was the incline. And that's when it dawned on me: running is a great metaphor for life. I was coasting along, oblivious to the things helping me at the time. I was taking it all in my stride, happy with my lot, and then I turned around and BOOM—adversity hit.

Suddenly, I wasn't going to be under 25 minutes for the 5-kilometre run—I'd be lucky to finish. The wind was making me feel like I was walking. My lungs screamed as I struggled to maintain my pace, and my legs burned from the incline.

My mind started coming up with excuses that would allow me to give up and just walk home: I'd done deadlifts and overhead squats at 5 am that morning; all I'd eaten since then was bacon and eggs and a protein shake; it was hot and I hadn't had enough water; I shouldn't kill myself now, but survive to run another day. So many excuses to just give up. Then a frame of reference from my mental bank kicked in.

It was a day in the Gumbad Valley like any other, except that a huge Taliban force had pinned us down. We had no food, no water and ammunition was scarce, with no hope of a resupply. I had to get my men out of that situation; giving up simply wasn't an option. That day had truly sucked. My run had nothing on that.

With that in mind, I convinced myself to keep running. I rolled through 3 kilometres in 5:21, with an average heart rate of 183 beats per minute. This run was now hard going, like life is sometimes. It had been easy for a while but now it was tough, but I knew it would become easy again in time, so I endured.

The wind became a surmountable challenge: I just decreased my stride and looked down. The incline wasn't an issue if I leaned into it and relaxed my breathing and legs. I rolled through the 4-kilometre mark in 5:46, heart rate 183 beats per minute. I was putting in a big effort, but I wasn't uncomfortable because I'd accepted that I would go through this hard patch. Doing so would increase my fitness and my character—I'd grow as a person.

I started to drift off, forgetting the pain. I looked around, at the plants in the sand dunes and the cars going past on the road nearby. I finished the last kilometre in 5:37, and my average heart rate was 186 beats per minute. It hadn't been easy.

Once I finished, I asked myself: *What would you do now if you were told to do it all again? Would you break? Or would you smile and nod, show little emotion and get the job done?*

Some parts of life are amazing. For the most part, though, life is mundane: it's comfortable and tolerable. But sometimes life truly sucks. It is punctuated by grief, sorrow and loss, and you have to dig deep just to endure it. The thing is, as I discovered on that 5-kilometre run, there are outside influences that affect your performance. Some of them you can contend with, and even use to your advantage; others you just have to roll with and endure. The trick is in understanding that this is occurring, and adapting your efforts to accommodate it. This knowledge might help you run your best 5-kilometre time, or maybe even make your life more worth living.

———

One of the most overlooked tools that can help us develop toughness is visualisation. In the 1990s, Lieutenant Colonel Dave Grossman researched the effects of visualisation and exposure to stimulus that reflected combat, and how this translated to making a person have a 'bulletproof mind'. As it applies to toughness, visualisation can pay huge dividends if done correctly. It's both an inoculation to a future event and a ready reckoner for making good decisions in the present.

Colonel Grossman was one of my leadership heroes. He was a West Point psychology professor, a professor of military science and an Army Ranger who had combined his experiences to become the founder of a new field of scientific endeavour that has been termed 'killology'. After discovering his work, I just had to know more, to understand how to train my men better and how to make sure they didn't get PTSD. I would do this by making sure they were ready for the effects of combat.

As a platoon leader, after delivering orders to my men I would spend an inordinate amount of time conducting war games. Initially, I did this for the guys, to develop the plan further. But over time I realised that what I was doing was getting their input into what might occur in the battle space. I was visualising the second- and third-order effects of my decisions and they were all living these different scenarios in vivid colour in their heads.

On a few of our missions the plan changed mid-operation because, hey, the enemy gets a vote too. But it didn't matter to me, as I had branches and sequels to the plan already worked out. I had visualised what I would do next. In fact, I had lain awake at night plotting my enemy's demise, and had knockout blows prepared for whatever they did. I respected my counterpart, but I also vowed never to get caught off guard.

One day, as we were moving along a quiet Afghan road—actually, we were well off to the side; we weren't stupid. The Bushmaster in front of me suddenly disappeared in a cloud of dirt and rock, and the percussion rocked my vehicle from side to side. When the dust cleared, the Bushmaster in front of me was facing my vehicle. It was missing its front wheels and the equipment bins off the side. The driver was mouthing a scream, but I couldn't hear him through the armoured glass.

Moments before, I had been visualising my response to this happening. I knew the area and I knew the enemy. Within seconds, I had delivered battle orders to the platoon and two teams from the rear of the convoy mobilised and rounded up some Taliban fighters in a building to our south-east. They had been watching us, and I had visualised that they presented the most likely threat.

Our medical response was just as fast. My platoon sergeant, Paul Cale, also used visualisation to pre-empt our enemy, so our decision-making cycle was faster than theirs. It meant that sometimes we were able to fire first, or that we reacted so fast to what should have been an ambush that the enemy was left with no option but to withdraw. Perhaps the situation I perceived was nothing like the eventual reality, but it prepared me to react instantly—violently, in some cases—and catch him off guard.

I continue to use this skill today, in my civilian life. I don't see vehicles blowing up anymore, but I do visualise the second- and third-order effects of my decisions. I'm rarely caught off guard or frozen into inaction. On the contrary, I'm motivated to take positive action.

———

One of the key ways to develop mental toughness and increase your resilience is to 'embrace the suck'. To show you what I mean by this, here's an example.

In the early 1990s when I was a young lance corporal, I was in a team selected to represent the battalion in a military obstacle course competition. We trained and trained, but we knew we weren't as fast as the favourites, who were from our sister battalion. The night before the competition, it rained and the course became a quagmire.

Our section commander, Corporal Stephen McCaig, watched the favourites head off on their run through the course. When they finished, he jogged over to us and immediately ordered us to dive into the mud at our feet and roll around. We looked at each other in quiet protest, but we had to comply. I thought he was being a jerk. Then it was our turn and we smashed the other team's time.

Our commander's reasoning was that the other team had approached the course tentatively, subconsciously trying not to get too dirty until they were halfway through. We were filthy before we'd even started, so we hit every obstacle hard. We didn't care that it was wet and muddy: we had already overcome that hurdle.

Ever since then, I've embraced the suck. If something is bad, I turn to others and say, 'How good is this?' Even if you're being sarcastic in the face of a challenge, it changes your perspective. The harder something is, the better the life experience to be gained.

That's the way I train now too. If it's freezing cold, I go for a swim. If it's super hot, I head out for a run. If it's blowing a gale and raining hard, I go for a ride. If someone better than me wants to train and make it a competition, I go into it looking to win, because in my mind there is only winning or learning. Other people's pain and negativity is like fuel for me.

Your mind holds the key to how you deal with life's challenges. Life isn't about sheltering from adversity and struggle. On the contrary, it's about embracing the hard times and owning them with a positive mindset. Change your perspective. Say out loud that something is going to be brilliant even if you know it's going to suck. Enjoy the moment you're in, because ultimately all your moments will run out.

LESSONS

Toughness is not fitness, but good fitness helps. We can train ourselves to do physically demanding tasks under moderate conditions quite easily.

The fitter you are, the less you have to rely on your mental toughness.

It takes considerably more effort to do the same tasks to the same standard in more demanding conditions, or an environment you're not used to. You have to train for this aspect of your toughness—there's no other way. Do arduous activities in arduous conditions.

When your physical toughness runs out, you have to rely on your mental resilience to work to a high standard in an unfamiliar environment. Such resilience is what sets high performers apart. They become the person to follow, and drive others to higher standards and accomplishments.

OPTIMISATION

9

ORGANISE YOUR CHAOS

'Simplify things, don't make them simpler.'

Albert Einstein

The Army is full of complexity, and dealing with complexity requires robust systems. When designing these robust systems for managing complexity, thought needs to be given to the design, ensuring there are easy to follow processes. Being well organised, personally and collectively, is vital to high performance. I had to learn this the hard way.

In the first few years of my career, I had a pack and webbing and a green military trunk. Inside this trunk I was required to keep all my deployment equipment. There were four pairs of green socks and two uniforms. I had a cups canteen—a stainless-steel, kidney-shaped cup with a folding handle that fits snuggly around a military water bottle in a purpose-designed pouch. One of the kidney cups was for shaving, another for tea, a pan set for messing, and a knife, fork and spoon set. I also had 10 metres of spare hoochie cord (3-millimetre braided nylon cord), a pair of sneakers and my Army physical training kit.

My pack always contained the same things: an entrenching tool (a folding shovel) for digging holes, four days' rations, six litres of water, a spare uniform in a garbage bag, a sleeping bag, a hoochie, my shaving kit, spare socks (again water-proofed), and anything my section commander wanted me to carry—usually a Claymore mine and a 66-millimetre rocket launcher. As a forward scout, I would also have a pace counter, a pair of secateurs, a bush saw and all my ammunition. Oh, and a Millbank bag for straining dirty water, which in two decades I never saw anyone use.

It felt like there was a lot to remember. But in the battalion, I spent most of my time downstairs in the breezeway, standing in a line holding pieces of equipment above my head, proof that I did indeed have the item called out from the deployment list. (I can sense other ex-soldiers shuddering at the thought of this.) Losing any of the issued equipment meant extra duties, so our incentive was to keep our weekend free.

When we deployed to Somalia in 1993, our packs and webbing came with us. There wasn't room for the trunk, though, so we put some spare things in a green echelon bag, which followed us separately. By the time I was reunited with mine, some four or five weeks later, I was in desperate need of a fresh uniform—and especially socks. Even then, it still seemed like I had lots to keep organised. I was nineteen years old, living out of my pack and webbing, and yet I didn't realise that this was as simple as my life would ever be.

We'd go out on patrol and come back to our platoon tent, where I rearranged my pack and webbing and then cleaned everything and rearranged it again. I was getting ready for the arrival of more stuff; it was sort of like I was nesting.

Wearing the same uniform for the better part of a month might seem extreme, but if you think about it, compared to World War Two this timeframe was short. Even so, I wonder how many people in this day and age have had to endure this small hardship. A weekend away camping is hardly the same as a month of patrolling in the same clothes, day and night. This experience gave me an early frame of reference, reinforcing for me that things usually aren't too bad.

I can pinpoint the phase of my career when my mind became sharper—when I became a smarter human, so to speak. It wasn't long after I started out in Special Forces, and corresponds with the time that I began to be responsible for more equipment. Instead of just a pack, webbing and metal trunk, I had two packs, three sets of webbing, a green plastic trunk with my deployment equipment, a green plastic trunk with my specialist role equipment, including my amphibious gear and my roping gear. I also had three personal weapons (two rifles and a pistol), and soon after doing the sniper course I would have five, adding two sniper rifles (one fully silenced).

None of this was superfluous—it was all mission-critical, to ensure that we had a collective capability. There was green role war-fighting equipment and black role counter-terrorist equipment. I had climbing and mountain warfare equipment, and when I became an officer I had platoon specialist equipment too.

All this equipment wasn't just dumped in the trunks: I had Velcro on the underside of the lids of my trunks, where I stored items that I needed regularly, such as torches, knives, magazines for weapons, and GPS watches. Other things were taped together, some in colour-coded sacks. My maps were in a small mapholder, with specialised pens and navigational items all together. Rubber bands, too, were a mainstay of my organisational life. Cords were rubber-banded to stop them tangling, ropes and slings were either taped or banded together—even my spare rubber bands were banded together.

I started to accrue more responsibility as well. My role now included writing directives, developing equipment submissions, conducting performance and counselling reports or auditory requirements—in short, all the tasks required of a person managing a platoon. Being responsible for all this equipment, and for the careers and wellbeing of my soldiers, as well as developing and then running their training, improved my ability to keep track of things. I developed systems for tracking equipment and tasks, and of course I learnt to access important pieces of knowledge quickly.

Nowadays, I'm often asked how I can have so many projects on the go at any one time. At one point, not long after leaving the Army, I was doing my normal day job, driving for two hours each way, completing a university undergraduate degree and a graduate diploma at the same time, while also writing my first military thriller, *The Fighting Season*. This was on top of being a new father and trying to maintain my fitness, as well as being the glue that was keeping my friendships relevant.

The truth is it's bloody hard to have so many things going on. I was drowning for a while there, and I often felt like I'd taken on too much and was never doing any of it to the best of my ability.

I think this is evident in the ending of my second book, *Off Reservation*, which was written during an emotional and chaotic time in my life. I rushed through it in order to get one of my priorities out of the way, but as a result I wasn't happy with the finished product. Writing fiction is something I really enjoy doing, but I did it in a rush rather than enjoying the process. Treating it as a chore made it harder work than it needed to be—and even when it was over I was still overworked and rushing other things.

When I reflected on this time, I realised that not long after departing service life, I had stopped using robust systems and had started letting tasks rule me.

I recalled the giant whiteboard that I kept in my platoon office: each line of text was printed using a ruler to keep the lines straight. On the left of the board was a long list of 'To Dos', broken up into immediate tasks ('A tasks'), this week's tasks ('B tasks') and this month's tasks ('C tasks'). In the middle of the board was a calendar showing upcoming events and important dates, and on the right of the board was a list of tasks that I had delegated to my soldiers, with a date to check on their progress and the completion dates.

It's important to understand that any board or system like this requires you to own it. The magic is not so much how the board organises your tasks, but how you interact with it to gain an under-standing of the tasks at hand. The secret is that it's your engagement that makes the board effective: writing down a new task, giving it a new priority, ticking a box or rubbing out a completed task. Standing in front of the board each day, preferably at a fixed time, studying it and getting cognitive buy-in—that's what makes it such a powerful tool.

However, a single whiteboard won't make you effective. When you try to multitask but have too many and varied priorities, it's easy to become overwhelmed. Multitasking within the framework of a system helps to maintain workflow and progression. Consideration should be given to the technologies and techniques that make your life easier, and to cutting away those tasks and habits that either create friction in your life or steal time away from you. You need to be prioritising the right things and doing them properly.

———

When I finally acknowledged that I was time-poor, I developed some tricks and techniques, based on my military experience, for managing my time and for managing my projects. I wish I'd recorded these years ago, rather than having to discover them for myself all over again. These tips and tricks might work for you too—although I hasten to add that we all have different things going on, and my way of doing things might not work as well for you. Inevitably it is contextual, so a bit of trial and error is required.

Firstly, review where your time is going by auditing a week of your life. You need to ascertain exactly how much of your time is swallowed up by things that aren't important. Your time is your most critical resource, and you need to understand where it is going.

I often use my calendar on my iPhone to track my life for a week to see where all the time goes, and from there to think about how I could use it better. From this analysis I change the way I do things.

Take the time to reconstruct your time use in detail. For example, think about the impact that living further from work has, or the distance you are from your kids' school—all those hours spent on public transport or in the car. If you have no choice about that, then work out how to best use that time. When I drove two hours each way to work, I educated myself on all manner of things—podcasts and audiobooks can be a great resource. Conversely, I have lived five minutes' walk from my work too, and this allows for more productive time in the office, and more time to train in the mornings.

I much preferred living close to work. When the kids came along, we realised that they too needed their time managed, especially when the after-school activities began. The closer you live to your work and school, the easier it is. Of course, there's an argument for having a better lifestyle on the weekends by being further out of the big cities—it all has to be weighed up. Either way, once you have your home location determined, it's all about using your time effectively.

Here's an example. Right now, I'm on a plane to Canberra for a wedding and I'm writing this on my iPad. When I land, I'll upload it to my WarriorU blog, and I'll save it as a Word document so I can expand on it for my next book (which you're now reading). Gary Vaynerchuk calls this technique creating silo content. I may also be able to use some of it on Twitter, Instagram or Facebook. So while I'm actually writing content for my book, it's feeding into the other projects that I have on the go. This is one example of getting bang for your buck when you're developing content; I'm multitasking without really even trying.

When you have multiple projects on the go, it's really important that you have good systems in place to manage all that knowledge. If you're messy with your data, it makes life all the harder. Filing systems are important: mine is based on what I developed in the military.

Over the years I've tried all sorts of storage and workflow solutions. In fact, I've probably helped numerous tech startups get the break they needed just by being an early adopter of their file management technologies. Most haven't worked for me; right now I'm using good old Dropbox, which I have on all my devices.

Evernote is another great resource. I use it as a type of personal search engine of all my documents. It's capable of so much more than that, but I tend to just save things to it so that I can easily find them again—including receipts and other tax-related documents. What makes it special is the tags, which let you group documents together. You can be as strict with these as you like, but if you have a good grasp of tags and can show a bit of discipline in how you save things, the program will be worth your time and effort. It's a great way of organising chaos.

We have a busy household, between my work, my wife's work, the kids' school activities, training every day. So I also use a PowerPoint slide to keep myself on point for the week. It's a single slide broken into quadrants, and represents a seven-day calendar. I break each day into hours, and then schedule physical training, work, meals, kids' activities and so on. It's not easy to construct it initially, but that's half the point: it's almost like a type of journaling for the week ahead, a project plan of my life for the next seven days. It's similar to the whiteboard concept, in that the magic lies in my interaction with the slide.

As well as having data management and calendars, I also try to outsource tasks that I don't have time for, or that I'm not very good at. Tim Ferriss's book *The 4-Hour Work Week* energised me: I was thrilled that someone had written this approach down and proclaimed it to be where the world is heading. I am hugely impressed by the young entrepreneurs who have cottoned on to the idea that time management is the next great frontier. I love exploring web-based tools or social media platforms that solve problems. Paying someone to write my blog, or having someone else edit my podcasts or my book allows me to make best use of my time, but it also gives me a social experience akin to developing a new friendship.

I strongly believe that structure helps us rein in complexity. Your systems and processes can be tailored to the life you want to lead. Once you've taken stock and worked out where your time is going, and what is most important to you, you can enjoy the fun part: building the life architecture that will allow you to be successful and manage the chaos of life. Remember, everything has a place, and you can put everything in its place.

LESSONS

Good organisation precedes consistently good performance. This is true not just of physical items, but also of our everyday lives.

The most productive people and organisations are masters of time management. Often, necessity drives effective time management, but you can beat the curve by applying concepts that save time across multiple disciplines.

Prioritise what you want to achieve, and make the most of the time you have available to you. Use your commute to work for learning, or your training time for social engagement.

Make use of programs, devices and systems that can maximise your time management at work and at home; the trick is to find the correct one for your circumstances.

10

TRAIN LIKE YOU FIGHT

'When it comes to the jungle, or life for that matter, learn
to play the game, because it's already playing you.'

There's an old saying that you should 'fight like you train'. But I prefer
the opposite: 'Train like you fight.' And nowhere is this more evident
than in the jungle, where every day is a fight against the elements
and your own complacency. It's an environment that forces you to
be thorough, and to observe important principles and routines. You
only break the rules in the most unusual circumstances.

Arguably, jungle warfare is the hardest type—perhaps not
between nation-states, but certainly at the personal level. So much
in the jungle is dead or dying, and it wants to take you with it. If it's
not decomposing, it's almost certainly feeding on something that is.
The plants sting you, the insects bite you, the heat drains you, the rain
freezes you, and everywhere the darkness gives you a hint of what
awaits you after death: blackness.

My two best friends from my basic and recruit training were
Travis and Mark. We marched into the 1st Battalion of the Royal
Australian Regiment (1RAR) in September 1991. 1RAR had its
origins in the aftermath of World War Two: it began as the 65th
Battalion, and was made up of the occupation forces in Japan. The
unit has served in nearly every major conflict our country has faced
since, then including Korea, Malaya, Vietnam, Somalia, East Timor

and Afghanistan. 1RAR is now based in Townsville, and is part of the Australian Army's 3rd Brigade.

At the time we joined 1RAR, the battalion's companies had already completed their collective training that year, and the focus was on the individual. Reconnaissance, sniper, signals, mortars and other specialist courses were being run by the Support and Admin companies. We were way too junior to be offered a specialist course, and so found ourselves leaving the battalion as fast as we had arrived. We hadn't even met our section commander yet, and now we were going out into the field. We were ordered to pack our 'bush gear' and report the next morning at 9 am. It was my first report time in the Army that wasn't before breakfast. I felt like an adult.

We marched off to the battalion headquarters and met up with the driver.

'Righto, lads, throw your shit in the trailer and find yourself a seat,' the young lance corporal told us, clearly relishing the responsibility. 'We'll stop a few times for a piss break and maybe a pie or two.' He was a few years older than me, tall and lanky, and his arms were covered in tatts. He spat on the ground a lot, picked his nose between comments and walked like he was carrying two watermelons under his arms. I thought he was awesome.

All we'd been told the night before was that we were going to Tully. I had no idea what or where or who Tully was. One of the more senior soldiers told me later on the van ride that we were to fill spots within the enemy section up at the Jungle Warfare Training Centre, in Far North Queensland.

We headed off through the harsh Townsville landscape and beyond. Rocky escarpments and dry riverbeds dotted the countryside. Then, almost as if it had been designed that way, the dry grasses and dusty paddocks became green. We were following the coast north, so to our right were green islands and blue seas, and to the left sugarcane farms and huge hills with looming dark clouds. Soon we were seeing banana plantations as well. I remember jumping off the bus at a small seaside café and buying a chicken pie and a Coke. That was probably one of the first things I had been allowed to do for myself since joining the Army some nine months before.

Three hours later, our van and its trailer turned off the small road and ascended a dirt track. As if on cue, the rain started to fall. An old Queenslander home, the groundskeeper's, was on the left, and there in his backyard was a giant wild boar, locked up in an old rusty cage. He was pacing up and down, his snout churning up the mud as he grunted his displeasure at our arrival. He was enormous, like something you would see in a zoo.

The buildings, I was told, were largely unchanged from when they'd been erected some 30 years before—and they remain largely unchanged to this day. They were in a large clearing in the jungle, the road no more than hard-packed gravel and sand. The buildings were simply roofs supported by wooden beams and a lattice of planks, surrounded by lush grass and the jungle. The grand-daddy of the structures was known as the Tully Hilton, a two-storey building that I would come to know well over my years in the Army.

The Hilton was big enough for a company of soldiers to escape the rain. With a platoon to each room, more than 30 men would be cramped together, with just a metre between your stretcher and equipment and that of the next guy.

But you wouldn't care, because if you were in the Hilton that meant you'd finished the twelve-plus days out in the jungle; it was the last place you went after company jungle training. That metre of personal space, that stretcher bed and mozzie net, that open hot shower and even the communal soap were the most amazing things in the world. Pure luxury.

On this assignment, as the enemy section for the Tully courses, we were lucky enough to have better accommodation just up the hill. It was a similar design, but it had iron sheeting on the sides and slatted windows, meaning it was cyclone-proof and weather-resistant. I walked into the accommodation with my pack and echelon bag containing pretty much everything I owned in this world. Travis and Mark followed me in and we looked around.

Griffo, the corporal from the battalion who was in charge of the enemy section, greeted us at the door and directed us to where we would be staying. There it was, a steel bed with wooden dowel poles taped on each corner holding up a tattered old mozzie net, an Army blanket and a steel wardrobe. My home for the next three months.

During the next week, we went over the enemy program with the directing staff (DS). There was an ambush course starting the following Monday for officers and senior non-commissioned officers (SNCOs), as well as a scout/tracking course for the battalion's scouts.

In 1991 the DS were mostly Vietnam veterans. They seemed old and crusty to me, but they were probably in their fifties at the most. They showed us around the jungle tracks that we would need to walk around. We set up some jungle camps for the tracking course to come and find. We spent hours in the booby trap lanes, helping one of the veterans to set up man traps and other devices that would kill or maim. I took an unhealthy interest in this, and I suspect that my interest may well have saved my life many years later in Afghanistan.

One of the traps we set up involved anchoring a giant piece of bamboo, about 80 millimetres in diameter, to a large tree so that it projected across a track. Then it was bent back and secured by a trip wire to another tree. The trigger was a wire running across the track. The trap was very sensitive: once released, the bamboo would whip across the track at knee height. We tested it a few times, the shrill sound it made was sickening. I knew that if it was actually used in anger, the air would be filled with screams. The booby trap lane was a highly dangerous, creative place. And I loved it.

My first job as an enemy fighter was also memorable. By now we had spent a week getting to know the jungle. The ambush course had arrived that Monday morning, delivered by bus down the road in a parking area. Rob Langdon, a more senior soldier who had volunteered to play enemy, and I watched the soldiers disembark.

There was an air of doom about them. All of them would have known this place, as they were either senior soldiers with over five years' experience or junior officers with at least a year under their belt. Perhaps that was why they were so quiet.

The DS briefed them on the left and right of the arc of the course, nominated platoon commanders and then gave them a grid reference that they would have to be at for their first lesson.

In relative silence, the men threw their packs over their shoulders, assembled in two makeshift platoons and disappeared into the jungle, up the track known only as Heart Break Ridge. The cicadas started instantly as the first man entered the jungle, and didn't stop for ten days.

Rob and I moved back to the Tully camp and prepared our gear for the evening's activities. It was a simple task: at 11 pm we were to patrol down one of the tracks leading away from the Tully camp, and be ambushed by the course. They had been receiving ambush lessons all afternoon, and that evening the DS would place them in a perfect ambush location and go over the mechanics of it all. Then in the evening they would re-create the lesson. Simple.

Eleven pm came around and we started down the track. We knew the entry point into the jungle and where we would be picked up at the other end, but not the exact location of the ambush. The DS wanted to keep us in the dark so our reactions would be more realistic. We were each armed with a bamboo pole with a small Cyalume light stick taped to the end, the small spot of light just enough for us to see where each footstep would land.

A few hundred metres into the jungle, I felt that my awareness was heightened. Rod was on the other side of the track, and I sensed that he was now taking this seriously too. We had learnt patrolling during our initial employment training in Singleton, and we'd now spent a week in the jungle, tuning in.

Slowly we moved further into the darkness. The canopy above the path allowed a little of the night sky's light to penetrate it, but the darkness on either side of the track was deathly. I crept forward and peered into the blackness, my heart rate had slowed right down and my movements were deliberate.

A few metres to my left, something caught my attention: it was a man lying in the undergrowth, his bush hat creating a straight edge that was out of place amid the curves of the jungle vines. I could only just make it out. I could have put my hand down and touched him, he was that close.

He didn't lift his eyes to look at me, but just stared at the ground in front of the barrel of his rifle. I could hear his breathing. The bloke next to him, too. It was the right-hand early warning of the ambush.

Their role was to communicate our presence with a hoochie string (a communications cord) that we had moved past. They would let the platoon commander, in the killing group, know that we were on our way into the killing ground of the ambush. Three tugs signified that we were on our way, and then a single tug thereafter for every enemy who was coming past.

I knew the killing group would be 50 metres further down the track, and I kept creeping on. Rob and I had long forgotten that this was training, and our movements became slower and even more deliberate. The silence was deafening; my heart pounded in my ears. After what felt like a lifetime, we covered another 40-odd metres.

Rather than initiate the ambush with his own rifle, or even a whistle that would alert the machine guns, the platoon commander pulled hard on the long wire attached to a trip-flare that had been secured in the ground with a small metal stake. Rob and I hit the deck as the flare was yanked out of the ground and through the undergrowth. They had left the pin in, and the flare failed to illuminate us.

No shooting started up, but we heard some cursing and yelling, and then the DS screamed at them: 'Start firing, for fuck's sake!' Rob and I jumped up and ran off down the track, at speed, all the way to the pick-up point. Then they started shooting.

I learnt a few things that day, and plenty more in the months and in the years that followed. I've been on the receiving end of many an ambush delivered by the Taliban, and they were up there with the best.

Firstly, if you're going to initiate an ambush, or any fight at all, go hard with everything you have and maybe you'll win. An ambush is a delicate thing: it needs to be crafted with the precision and the care of an artist. But it also needs to be initiated with the brutality of an MMA fighter. You can't set it off with the platoon commander's rifle, or a whistle or a light. It needs to be initiated with a massive explosion—shock and awe, and lots of shooting. In fact, fuckloads more of it than you think you need. It has to be poured into the killing ground in murderous waves.

I also learnt that we all shoot way too high. Another fact is that men who have been shot become immune to being shot at; that is, they start to be able to operate even during the shock of an ambush— unless they're all dead at the start. The tables can be turned on you rapidly. I've also experienced this, and my advice is to carefully consider a break-contact plan.

Rob and I were driven back to the start of the course, and we headed off down the track again. This time we were instructed to take bigger torches, walk along the track side by side, and have our weapons up over our shoulders as we talked shit to each other. We got to the killing ground and the ambush was initiated by a block of explosives and then rifle fire, closely followed by the two guns on either side of the group. We lay down and let the men do their business; they searched us, and I remember receiving a solid kick in the nuts for fucking them around earlier in the evening.

Eventually the platoon commander gave the command to withdraw, and they drifted off into the jungle. We heard the rustling of leaves and a few curses as guys got caught up on wait-a-while vines. All in all, they did a great job, and they got a lot better over the next two weeks as Rob and I shadowed them as their enemy.

When I was a platoon commander, many years later, I trained my men to always stay in the fight—they were to keep engaged with the Taliban at all costs, to pursue them so they couldn't move. That might seem counterintuitive or lacking in common sense, but it was highly successful for us. Staying engaged with the enemy on our terms enabled us to gain and retain the initiative until the job was done. We could dictate the pace and rhythm of the engagement, the ground it was fought over and the final act of completion or disengagement. It meant that those involved in the firefight would often take off in quick pursuit, while I manoeuvred my men to flank the enemy somewhere else.

This tactic works when your men all know the standard operating procedures (or SOPs): they drop smoke to show their direction of movement and they continue to radio their locations and directional headings based on a ground reference guide. While my platoon was doing its best to maintain the engagement, I would be going through my 'OODA loop'—a continuous decision-making process whose framework is *observe–orient–decide–act*—and trying to get inside my adversary's OODA loop at the same time. My goal would be to conduct my decision-making at a faster rate, so as to keep him on the back foot.

The OODA loop is based on the idea that to be successful in combat, you need to make good decisions quicker than your opponent. Firstly, you need to *observe* everything going on around you, using all your senses. This includes the amount of fire incoming, the number of civilians in the town, the time of day or night, the number of enemy aircraft and so on. With your observations complete, you then *orient*, or shape, the data to form a complete picture of the situation. Your mental perspective will also be informed by your previous experiences, which can create a thinking bias, and—if you are smart—the opinions of those around you whose input you trust. Next you *decide* on the best course of action, which may mean rejecting other courses of action. Lastly, you need to *act* on that decision. Your action draws a reaction from your adversary, which you observe—and the process starts again. The cycle repeats continuously while you're engaged in the activity. The aim is to force your adversary's reaction, and prevent him from forcing a reaction by you, until you either defeat him, get him to disengage or otherwise achieve your desired end state.

The jungle forces each soldier to go through the OODA loop continuously. You are frequently out of sight of most of your eight-man section, much less your 30-man platoon. You are repeatedly visually isolated from your nearest partner and so must use voice and sound to coordinate your efforts, and this requires you to orientate to the situation on your own. You must decide on the best course of action available to you as quickly as you can, and then act upon it to force your adversary to make a decision. If you have done your job right, it enables you to win the day.

The jungle was a great teacher and often in the Green Belt of Afghanistan we would find ourselves in thick vegetation that would make the operating environment more akin to North Queensland than the Middle East. My platoon won every firefight where we maintained the rage from initial contact; conversely, in the early days, more often than not we were forced to withdraw when we tried to take our time to orientate ourselves.

Room combat was a little bit different to back in Australia as well. For starters the shapes of the doors and the windows weren't the same. The layouts of the buildings were unusual to us at first. There were often courtyards in the middle of the *qualas* (compounds) and there would be animals walking around, including chickens and dogs and goats. We set up our own enemy compound and we would attack it through the day and then we would attack it at night. We bought goats and chickens from a market and put them inside the building as well, and then we would attack it again. We dressed people up as locals and made these actors rush at us while we came through the doors or over the walls. We would attack it and attack it again until we could do it perfectly. We were training in the way we would fight.

LESSONS

Whatever the circumstances, you have to train like you're going to fight.

You have to train to be able to make decisions under immense pressure—it's a perishable skill that can expire over time.

You have to train to reinforce success so that you're ready when you need to do it. Conversely, you have to train not to reinforce failure.

If you find yourself constantly reacting in a fight, then you have to be prepared to change the way you're fighting.

By all means use this as a guide, but it's only that. Be creative.

11

HABITS REINFORCE DISCIPLINE

'Watch your habits, they become your character . . .'

Frank Outlaw

We've seen how laziness can become a habit, and how important it is to try to identify this within oneself. Laziness is opposed to discipline. The more disciplined a person becomes, the more they can control most facets of their life. Ultimately, discipline gives a person the freedom to break free of societal chains and cultural restrictions.

This isn't my unique thought, nor is it the unique thought of some bestselling Navy Seal commander—it's contained throughout various historical teachings, notably from Buddhism. It stands to reason that the more energy you need to invest in decision-making, the less freedom you have. Freedom is the experience of not being reactive to vast amounts of choice, and this takes discipline.

Self-discipline can be developed and strengthened when we support our behaviour with good habits. People don't have a never-ending reserve of self-discipline, so it's important to understand that habits can be an effective means of stopping us from deviating from our mission or succumbing to temptation. There is real power in saying NO.

However, self-discipline doesn't just materialise in someone's personality. On the contrary, it requires consistent practice. In most cases, the development of self-discipline requires a person to bend their own will, to conduct introspection and to identify that they need to increase their willpower. The good news is that willpower can be increased gently, over time, if you know what you're doing. It can be done by slowly increasing the number of good habits in your life.

I have seen and experienced how the Army increases a recruit's self-discipline. Firstly, the institution imposes its will on the recruit and makes them accountable; then the recruit sees the benefit of getting things done without being asked; and over time they see the massive benefit of self-discipline. Civilians can slowly increase their own self-discipline in the same way.

My Army experience taught me that I needed self-discipline in order to avoid too much choice. I realised that I had to incorporate a mixture of the following habits into my life: hygiene habits, daily non-negotiables, weekly organisation habits, and what I call toughness habits in order to strengthen the self-discipline habits I was developing.

Most of us learn hygiene habits from our parents or caregivers from an early age. In the Army, these are forced on you from your first day, and they're expected just about every day thereafter. Generally speaking, hygiene habits should be automatic and shouldn't take any intellectual energy. If they're not already part of your daily routine, then I beg you, for your own sake and the sake of those around you, start developing them now. If you're not doing half of these already . . . well, you probably stink.

- Make your bed first thing, every single day.
- Fold the clothes you wore to bed and place them under your pillow.
- Shave every morning, or at least wash your face and tidy your hair.
- Wear deodorant.
- Brush your teeth once in the morning and once in the evening; floss.
- Wear clean underwear and socks every day.
- Bathe or shower daily.

You probably do most of these on most days. There are days when you don't, of course, because you're on holiday (or on patrol), but that's okay: you're making a conscious decision to take a break from your good habit. You shouldn't have to think too much about hygiene habits, and they don't require much self-discipline. You're on autopilot. This just goes to show the strength of a good habit.

A non-negotiable is a habit that you will not compromise on. These are the powerful things that set you apart from those who bitch and moan about their lives. Non-negotiables are the daily habits that allow you to manage your time efficiently and be productive. They include things like:

- Sleep for at least eight hours, every night.
- Get up early and go to bed early. I'm up at 5 am every weekday, so for me that means bed and sleep by 9 pm each night.
- Conduct all hygiene habits.
- Use the early part of the day for an activity that force-multiplies your time, such as meditation, yoga, sauna, range-of-movement exercises, weight training, running, swimming, journaling, group fitness class. Anything that gives your body and soul an advantage. Get it done and get on with your day.
- Morning reflection; for me this involves a coffee and sitting down to write a work plan and a timeline for the day.
- Get ready to leave the house, and then empty the kitchen bin. Also, ensure the dishwasher and the washing machine are on. By doing this you're using the appliances for the purpose they were designed for, saving you time.
- Travel to work and listen to a podcast. I recommend *The WarriorU Podcast*! But I also like *The School of Greatness* by Lewis Howes and *The Joe Rogan Experience*. Or listen to a university lecture, an audiobook or the news. It's about self-development. In most cases, listening to commercial morning

radio only ensures that you're receiving paid advertisements or the opinions of people who, in the grand scheme of things, probably aren't worth listening to.

- Upon arriving home, empty the dishwasher and the washing machine.
- Decompress from work when you get home. That could mean going for a run or walking the dog.
- Spend focused time with the kids. Allow no compromise: give them your full attention.
- Prepare the evening meal; make extra for lunch the next day, or freeze for a meal for another week.
- In the evening—at 8 pm in my house—we turn off the internet at the same time every day. That means no Facebook or other social media!
- Lay out clothes for the next morning's gym session.
- Pack lunches and bags for the coming day's activities. Prepare to own the next day.
- Read a chapter of a book before bed, or read a book with your children.

Make all these good habits non-negotiables, and hit as many of them as you can each day until you are habitually doing them all. If you can achieve this, you won't need anywhere near as much self-discipline for other things. Life happens, and your sense of freedom will increase because you're not stressed by it all. You can schedule your free time because you have created it.

Weekly organisational habits are those things that we do once a week to set ourselves up for success. These are the habits and behaviours that do the heavy lifting: the tasks that set the tempo for the rest of the week, and ultimately will support you to thrive, as opposed to just survive. For my family, these activities generally occur on the weekend.

- Saturday-morning breakfast with the kids. This is when we create a meal plan for the week, taking into account each person's schedule, activities and dietary needs.
- Saturday-morning weekly shop. Armed with the meal plan, it's easy to conduct a major shop for the food you need for the week.
- Sunday meal prep. The weekly meal plan drives what this looks like. A lot of time during the week can be saved if food is prepared in advance and reheated.
- Create a weekly program for each person in the house, addressing their requirements for the week. We use a PowerPoint calendar that has a column per person (plus one for our dog!), outlining any major events for the week. Sport, school, meetings, travel, appointments—nothing should be a surprise.

Perhaps all this seems a bit prescriptive? My experience is that weekly organisational habits get easier and feel more natural each week. Over time, you'll get to know what works best for you, and your templates will become more meaningful and effective.

Toughness habits are those that require you to win a battle of wills with yourself. They're the small incremental things that you do that have powerful second-order effects when you do them for long enough. These habits will generally require much more self-discipline, and you need to practise them until they become part of your personality.

With the natural exception of mental health issues, being a stoic and suffering in silence can be a great way to build mental toughness. Start small and work your way up. When you order a coffee, only ever order the smallest one. Think about it—if you build this into a habit, then over time the reduction in your calorie intake will be massive.

The same goes for junk food. If you have no other option but to eat it occasionally, order only a small portion. Wear this like a badge of honour. When everyone else is ordering Big Mac meals and supersizing, you're having a cheeseburger, small fries and a water. That's your thing! If you're asked about it, you can say it's a habit you've developed—this helps reinforce it further.

Reducing your sugar intake until you can achieve no added sugar is another small habit that will have a big effect; the science on this is well known. It's safe for me to say that cancer feeds on glucose. Make it your toughness habit to not add sugar.

As I've already discussed, environmental impacts offer a great path to building mental toughness. I run in extremes—heat and storms are my favourites. Make it your toughness habit to use these extremes to your advantage. Or try having a 'push-up day'—I do this once a month. Every time I need to go into or out of the house, it's 100 push-ups. This might not seem like a habit, but it's definitely building your self-discipline. You will be fighting yourself to keep it up throughout the day.

You get the point. Toughness habits build a strong mind and body; weekly habits build structure; daily habits remove the need for so much self-discipline; and hygiene habits basically just keep your friends around. Ultimately, good habits reinforce discipline, and discipline leads to better time management. Good time management means you get the most bang for your buck in your short time here on earth.

———

Bad habits always seem more noticeable than good ones. Good habits help you develop discipline, and discipline makes you more effective. However, you must put in a certain level of effort and not just go through the process.

We've already met the phrase 'Prior preparation prevents piss-poor performance'. This is so very true. Most activities in the Army require some level of planning and preparation, and it's about more than just attendance. Applying yourself to a task is just as important a habit as any other.

One of the fundamentals of self-discipline is to focus on the process, not the outcome. When we focus on outcomes, we naturally try to protect ourselves from failure, but when we focus on the process, and all its component parts, a challenge becomes surmountable. Learning to toughen up and to do what's important is another aspect; that is, not taking the easy option. You have to learn to enjoy taking the hard right over the easy wrong.

When I first committed to becoming tougher, back in 1991, I decided that I would reward my self-discipline. I promised myself a treat, which I'd only receive when I had completed whatever the menial or difficult task was. But the best way to reinforce self-discipline, in my view, is to be an example to others. Don't feel you have to shout about it from the rooftops; quiet and persistent self-discipline doesn't go unnoticed.

On Army training courses, you're expected to fasten your pouches or zippers every time you take something out or put something in. The training staff are ever watchful. They scan the packs and bags that are lined up in neat rows. Each bag has a call sign clearly identifying the owner. Punishments for leaving a pouch undone range from burpees to pack marches, ensuring that soldiers develop self-discipline.

Why is it so important to fasten your pouches? For a number of reasons, one of the main ones being that the Army does not want its operators to lose mission-essential equipment while conducting a task. Most equipment used by Special Forces is expensive. Moreover, if something gets lost, it might aid an enemy, or even be used back against us. Also, not leaving anything behind that could be linked to your involvement in the operation is essential in some missions.

There's another reason too. The character of a person can be easily assessed by how they treat their equipment, and the state they leave it in. Not paying attention to the pouches, the zips and Velcro tabs demonstrates, at a fundamental level, either that their personal commitment to the task is poor, that they lack self-discipline, or that they have a weak mental disposition. Operators either don't realise that what they are doing is lazy and harmful to their performance, they don't care—which is actually worse—or they are unable to win the mental fight to rectify their behaviour.

So do up your bags and pouches. Create habits that make you efficient and effective. Develop the discipline to maintain these habits. Greater economy of effort will create time and space for you to use for work or pleasure. You will wake every day knowing you have a purpose. You will execute your daily tasks in good time and with precision. You will make good use of the time you have created, you'll go to bed confident that you've squeezed as much as possible into your day, and you'll be well prepared for the next one.

LESSONS

By organising your hours, days, weeks, months and year, you create structures to work within. If your lifestyle is busy enough, you will need habits if you want to keep doing certain things with regularity.

Some habits come easily, but others require more discipline—like getting up early and training hard first thing in the morning.

The key to maintaining good discipline is to make these things habits. They may seem routine but they will give you an enormous sense of self-worth. Achieving even the smallest things will make you feel you have accomplished something worthwhile, even if the rest of your day does not go to plan.

Focus on the process, not on the outcome. Outcomes cause us to fear failure, and it is only through failure that you'll learn what processes don't work.

If you look honestly at the procedures, habits and discipline that underpin your life, you'll gain the outcomes you desire.

12

LISTEN AND OBSERVE

'When people talk, listen completely.
Most people never listen.'

Ernest Hemingway

In the previous couple of chapters, I have argued that you need to make observations using all your senses in order to orient yourself and take quality decisions and actions. This might seem odd, given we're used to observing with our eyes, but as the OODA loop theory says, you need to merge the data from all your senses to gain a complete picture. True listening—as opposed to simply hearing—is very much a part of this process.

When I was sixteen years old, I was able to ride my bike further afield and also catch buses to all parts of the city. My range had increased, meaning I could explore beyond my immediate environment. I began working a few part-time jobs so that I could make a little money, which made it easier for me to chase girls. I was trying to live like an adult but was still too young to really understand the ramifications of any life decisions I made.

I also felt the urge to explore, to see the world and do something great with my life. Not unlike the Anzacs of yesteryear, my adventurous spirit was inflamed by stories of heroism in combat. Victoria Cross winners, the Falklands Islands conflict, the first Gulf War. The ads on TV for the Army were equally compelling: the bronzed Australian in the starched green uniform, pulling a yabby off his tank cupola after successfully navigating a water crossing and throwing it to his chef mate. 'Cook this up for us, Davo!' came the cry.

I'd never eaten yabbies, but I knew they must be delicious. I knew what I was going to do with my life: I'd join the Army and live on adventure and freshwater crustaceans. It would be glorious. But I was still too young, as I wouldn't be seventeen until October 1990.

I was in the first term of Year 12 at Banksia Park High School, but I had no idea what I was studying. The only subject I showed any promise in was English. I was at the bottom for everything else and couldn't care less. Then one afternoon I went to a rural job agency that had job cards pinned to a board in their window. Back in 1990, the paths people took in their lives had as much to do with happenstance as with planning or research.

I saw a job post for a station hand. I can't remember what it actually said, but I remember the feeling that came over me: I sensed adventure and discovery. This feeling would continue to drive the decisions I made in life from that day forward. Even today, every time I feel it something inside me awakens. I ripped off one of the paper tags and went home and talked to my father, and a few weeks later I took a Greyhound bus to a sheep station in Cocklebiddy, Western Australia.

I was taken under the wing of the station owner and his family. I think they were kind of shocked at how young I was when I arrived: there had been just one telephone interview, and then this 48-kilogram, sixteen-year-old boy turned up.

I worked hard, harder than I'd ever worked before, but probably not as hard as they expected. Coming from the city, I was yet to understand what true work was; as anyone who has worked on a sheep station will tell you, it's back-breaking. I learnt to drive on that sheep station, and I learnt to ride a motorbike there too. I learnt to kill beasts and skin them. In fact, my first lesson on listening became my first lesson on killing.

The station owner asked me to go and turn on the water tap for a trough in one of the far-off paddocks. It was a morning's motorbike ride to get there. When I arrived, I turned on the tap, checked the windmill to make sure it was pumping properly, then hopped on my bike and rode back to the station house. I had been told to stay and watch the sheep approach, and make sure they didn't stampede each other to get to the water as it had been a dry summer and they hadn't had water for a few days. But I was more concerned about the cup of tea and biscuits that would be on offer at 10 am.

I was yet to learn that while hearing is simply a function, true listening is a skill. It's important to listen to what someone is actually saying, not just hear their words as they talk. Listening is a key aspect of situational awareness: to listen is to try to comprehend, not just to react.

The next morning, I was summoned to the station owner's house. He exploded when I got there, yelling at me about the dead and dying sheep. He had done an early-morning drive around some paddocks and had come across the terrible scene. I hadn't listened to him properly, and the animals had rushed the water and trampled each other.

He slammed a knife on the table and the keys to a truck. 'Go and get the dead carcasses and load them on the truck. If any sheep are dying, you've got to kill and load them too.'

I was mortified. I couldn't drive a truck, let alone kill a sheep. Sure, he had shown me once, but I'd never thought I would have to do it. I went to the shed and climbed in the front of the big Ford truck. It had so many gears, and I didn't know how to change them properly. I drove in first gear for what felt like forever, until I remembered the lesson he'd given me about using the clutch. On the fourth attempt I managed to shift into second gear. I kept practising, changing gears as I went. Going down the gears was easy, but going up again was trickier. After a while I'd learnt to do it well enough to get the big truck moving at a decent pace.

When I arrived at the water trough, the scene was horrific. I saw more than two dozen carcasses, and another ten or more with broken legs or backs but still alive. I reversed the truck close to the dead and dying sheep.

I decided to kill the injured sheep first, and I remember crying as I killed the first one. I pulled its head back, but made the mistake of looking into its eyes. Stabbing the sheep in the side of the neck, I cut its throat, quickly severing its spinal cord. I started to cry more heavily as I went over to the next animal. I killed them all, then I dragged some dead animals out of the trough. The other sheep competing for the water had drowned them.

Next I started to load them onto the truck. They were heavy, weighing not much less than me; some of the flyblown ones weighed a lot more. I lifted them up onto the tray and their blood and fluids covered me. It was now midday, stinking hot and dusty. I was covered in sweat and blood and other crap. I sat on the ground and sobbed for a long while.

When I look back on this time now, I realise it was a turning point in my life. When I arrived back at the homestead I could drive a truck and I could kill an animal. More significantly, I had been responsible for the deaths of innocent creatures. The innocent and playful child in me had died that day; I was now a man—a young man, but a man nonetheless.

I had also learnt a very valuable life lesson: the importance of listening to instructions. My lack of humility, my failure to appreciate the importance of the task and my unwillingness to listen properly had landed me in a situation that I was not prepared for. It would not be the last time I would learn this lesson, and I'm sure I will learn it again. My goal is to keep these lessons further apart.

———

Observation is another important skill to master. We've all heard the old saying 'You can't see the forest for the trees'. This means that there's so much going on in the environment you're observing that you struggle to see the big picture. We've all been guilty of this in our lives, to varying degrees. We do it subconsciously, as a way of expediting things.

Think about filling out a form. Every now and then, one asks for your last name first and your first name last. We've all automatically filled in a form like this incorrectly—and it's okay, because it's human to do so. It is called a thinking bias.

Thinking biases exist at every level of our lives. They include what we expect a child to do when we ask them to keep their room clean, or how an employee is expected to complete a task, or the time of day we expect the sun to rise or set. You know these things and expect them to occur, based on your own experiences and expectations.

Psychologist and economist Daniel Kahneman has identified that people think in two different ways: fast and slow. The idea is that our human nature causes us to come to a conclusion almost immediately that we think will be right. He calls this 'thinking fast'. We often call it a gut instinct, and people pride themselves on their ability to think in this way and be proven right.

Many people will tell you how amazing it is that their gut instinct turns out to be right so often. The fact is they only keep score of the ones they get right. To borrow from Kahneman: what temperature does water boil at on top of Mount Kosciuszko? Your immediate response will likely be 100 degrees Celsius, but if you think about it more carefully, you might remember from high school science that the lower air pressure at altitude causes water's boiling point to be lower as well. This is your brain thinking slow, and it's how we challenge our thinking biases and come up with original thoughts and ideas.

Another good example of thinking biases comes from World War Two. During the US bombing campaign against Germany, there was significant loss of aircraft and life due to German anti-aircraft fire. The Americans decided to try to identify where the majority of shrapnel and bullets were striking the aircraft, and to put armour there to prevent damage. Good idea, right?

Then someone pointed out that the only aircraft they were assessing were the ones that had made it home. Really, the ones that hadn't made it home were the ones they needed to check for battle damage. Obviously, that couldn't happen, but it forced a reassessment of the thinking. The answer ended up being to armour the areas where there was *no* damage on the aircraft that had returned, as these were the vulnerable spots.

It's a good example of a group thinking fast initially, and then an individual taking a longer look at the problem and realising that they were 'solutioneering'. Their thinking bias had led them to focus on the aircraft that had survived instead of those that hadn't.

So now they had figured out the best spot to put the armour, the problem was solved, right? The armoured aircraft had to survive longer: they were now bulletproof. Well, bulletproof where they needed to be, anyway. The only problem was that *more* armoured aircraft were being lost than unarmoured aircraft, and no one could figure out why.

The armoured aircraft, it was eventually realised, were now heavier and slower, meaning they fell out of the formations and were easier targets for the *Luftwaffe*. Once again, the group thinking had failed: it did not recognise the second- and third-order effects of the armour. Just because it works well on a tank it doesn't mean it will work on a plane.

I once heard a rather gross saying about not moving quickly: 'If you were any slower, I could spit in your eye.' That's what happened to the up-armoured bomber aircraft. They were now so slow the *Luftwaffe* could pick them off one by one. Sometimes the obvious solution is not the best one.

Listen to people and the environment; don't just hear things. Eventually, the right solution will present itself. The trick is to act upon this solution when you recognise it.

LESSONS

Listening to what you are hearing is the gold standard, and helps you avoid getting things wrong. Listening is to hearing as observing is to seeing.

The same thing said to two different people can yield completely different results, because of the way we listen—or don't—and because of our thinking biases.

Thinking biases lead us to base our conclusions or decision-making on our previous experiences. We trick ourselves into thinking that our 'gut instinct' is almost never wrong.

The way to overcome a thinking bias is to step back and make a considered observation before making a considered decision.

13

THE POWER OF STORYTELLING

'Say what you mean and mean what you say.'

Anonymous

I witnessed so many meetings and conversations while in the Army, and particularly as an officer, and I was always amazed at how often people missed the points being raised by the other person in the conversation, or being confused because the two sides had a different interpretation of a word. I found it fascinating, too, that the main culprits were those lieutenant colonels who everyone called 'future Chiefs of the Army'. One Special Forces officer in particular was notorious for hearing only what he wanted, as educated as he was. He wasn't a great listener, and this made communication difficult.

A lot happens during a linguistic transaction, and one of the most important skills, as we've just discussed, is listening: paying real attention to the other person and accurately turning their words into a thought in your own mind. Have you ever had a meeting with someone who talks over you, or doesn't let you get a word in? What about the person who asks you a question and then looks away, focusing on something other than you? These people clearly lack a key linguistic skill. We know intuitively that they're not interested in us or what we are saying.

Conversations are made up of more than just the words we speak. A conversation also comprises facial expressions, hand gestures, turn taking and interjections. There's also the way we say things, our tone and the emphasis we put on our words. Concentrating on the other person and getting this right can be exhausting.

Many words can mean different things, depending on the context or the way they're used. Sometimes we use the wrong words by accident, which can change the meaning of the sentence completely and confuse the listener. Or a speaker uses the wrong words because they don't know the right ones; misinterpretation of the message is therefore likely.

Much of my Army career centred on conveying my intentions to subordinates, giving orders to soldiers, explaining the intricacies of a plan or briefing senior commanders. The words I used were as important as the way I said them. I learnt a few rules for giving orders. Firstly, always get to the point. Use language that's easy to understand—don't try to sound smart for the sake of it. If in doubt, talk about the end state you want to achieve, and describe the journey to get there using simple terms that clarify the result.

Learning to become a skilled communicator will unlock worlds that you didn't know existed. It will also encourage you to become more efficient and give your relationships greater depth and meaning.

The secret to being a skilled communicator is actually to become a skilled storyteller. It doesn't matter who you are—whether a commander, a business leader, a manager—what is intended isn't always what is heard. A communicator needs to analyse information, then disseminate it. Sometimes the message is the meaning; that is, the way we deliver the content might be just as important as the content itself. Let me give you an example.

The class comprised over 30 people. The tables in the room formed a hollow square, with the front edge missing. Students sat on the outside of the square, facing the giant screen, so they could all see the presentation. I walked into the hollow square and divided the students into teams. The left side was Team 1, the centre facing the screen was Team 2, and the right side was Team 3.

'Okay, listen up,' I began 'Each team has one minute to get together and choose a leader. Your time starts now.'

I watched the craziness begin. A time constraint, mixed in with uncertainty over who's in charge, always causes chaos—and makes me smile. Finally, after the world's shortest minute, the leaders of each team were decided. Having either volunteered or been press-ganged, they made their way to the front of the room.

I introduced myself to the three leaders, wrote their names on the board and then turned to face them. I hustled them in closer so that only they could hear me.

'What I want you to do now is go back to your teams. I want you to organise the tables into three different workstations. Each team is to sit around that workstation so that they can face each other, collaborate and solve a problem. Do you understand?'

The three nodded, and then I asked one of them to repeat what I wanted done. Satisfied that they had understood my instructions correctly, I let them go. The leaders returned to their teams and passed on the instructions, and the 30 people went about arranging their tables so that they were organised into the separate team areas. Once they were all seated, I regained the class's attention.

'The reason I organised you in to teams, and then had you nominate a leader, was so I could demonstrate that instructions are more easily conveyed and adhered to when a leader gives up responsibility for the whole group and assigns it to the leaders of smaller groups. I reduced my span of command to something more manageable. When you create a leadership structure, you are able to streamline your thoughts and directions.'

Everyone agreed that this created a much better way to organise the moving of the tables; it was less confusing and there was less fuss.

I'd learnt this technique early as an officer in the Special Forces. As a soldier, my platoon commanders would give me orders and I'd carry them out, but I never truly understood what was occurring until I was a platoon commander myself. As an officer, I worked out that yelling my intention to the masses not only exposed me to questions of fact, as well as the occasional protest, but it also often created confusion after an initial period of discussion. Calmly passing orders to my trusted junior leaders always—*always*—resulted in more controlled decision-making. They took ownership and sold my plan to their men.

I went around to each set of tables and got them working on their tasks. Once this was done, I had the leaders get up and present their deliverables. At the completion of these tasks, I wanted to get the group turned back around and facing the giant screen.

'Leaders to me,' I said, watching them as they rose from their seats and made their way forward. 'Okay, go back and brief your teams that I want to use these tables later for another activity, but for now I want the class to move their chairs into the centre of the room, between the tables, facing the screen so they can see the presentation. Are there any questions?'

The three looked at me and shook their heads, and I sent them back to the groups.

I kept an eye on the leader of Team 1 as he complied. 'He wants us to move our chairs to the centre of the room,' the man said to his group members, and I heard exasperation in his voice.

Bingo, I thought.

The teams arranged their chairs, and I waited until they were all seated. Then I asked one of the guys from Team 1 to come to the front. 'What did your team leader ask you to do,' I said, smiling.

'He asked us to move our chairs to the centre of the room.'

'What else did he say? What reason did he give for that to occur?'

'He didn't say anything else. Just that.'

'Alright, you can sit down, mate.'

I tuned to the audience and called out the leader of Team 1. 'What did I tell you to do?'

'Ah, you told us to go back and brief our teams that we would use these tables again and that we now needed to move the chairs to see the screen.' I could see he knew already what the teaching point would be.

I asked him to sit down again, and then I gave the class a few seconds to think about what had just happened.

'Generally, an instruction between a leader and their subordinates has different parts. In this instance, there was a clear instruction, but I also gave a clear reason. My instruction also included a warning order for another task—that the chairs were going to be moved back later on.' I let that sink in for a few seconds. 'Moreover, the way the team leader passed the information on made it appear that we were doing it just for the sake of it. His communication style didn't support me as a leader. Here I am, providing a justification which makes perfect sense, and he just passed on the basic instruction, as if it was pointless and unnecessary. Actually, I wanted you to move so you were more comfortable facing the screen. I could have asked that we set the class up in the square configuration again, but as the leader I decided this would just be making more work for you.'

The class got it. It had seemed like I was stuffing them around, but the truth was I had their best interests at heart. But this point hadn't been understood and conveyed.

When a leader passes information to their subordinates for wider dissemination, it's vital that the true essence of the communication is conveyed. Subordinates who find themselves in leadership positions need to take great care with what they pass on. A leader's intent generally consists of their reasoning or justification as well as the task or instructions. A leader can be made to look bad when a subordinate leader chooses which part of the instruction or task to pass on to the wider team, and which part is left out.

The leader must also take responsibility—ownership, if you will—for what they say and how they say it. It's vital that the leader understands their subordinates, as it helps them decide how much detail to go into. Some people may need you to outline the specifics of a task and exactly what must be conveyed; others might intuit your intent and then provide all the information that you want them to, plus more. As a leader, you have to think about this. If your intent wasn't made clear, then it was probably your own style that was the problem.

Before you pass on information, think deeply about what it is that you want to say, what your intent is for the task, and whether other, perhaps future, tasks might be left out of what you are asking.

———

It could be argued that modern humans owe our existence to our ability to tell stories. Perhaps we were better at this than Neanderthal man. There's certainly a correlation between the explosion of human development across the globe and our ability to preserve knowledge. Indeed, there's scientific evidence to show that we retain information better when we write things down or draw them, so using mind-mapping techniques and whiteboards to convey ideas may be just as valuable as writing them down.

Imagine, for a moment, a group of *Homo erectus*, sitting together in a cave on a warm summer's evening on the edge of the African savannah. They are huddled around a small fire at the entrance of the cave, more for protection than for warmth. Their bellies are full because that day they'd tracked an animal to exhaustion and then hacked at its flesh and brought back piles of meat for the small community. It was a feast.

One of the older men speaks to the others. 'Out there, in the dark, is an animal. It has two huge front teeth and red eyes, and if you wander too far from here, alone, before the light is halfway up in the sky, this animal will eat you.'

Perhaps this communication would have been made in guttural utterances, but the image would have been vivid and terrifying for the people of the tribe. Perhaps the story was replete with drawings on the wall of the cave, and then added to over time—like a primitive PowerPoint presentation.

In fact, it would probably have been delivered better than many PowerPoint presentations are today, with presenters relying on 'slide-ology' to compensate for their poor presentation style. PowerPoint has a tendency to remove from the speaker the burden of remembering their story and articulating their point or opinion appropriately; it can serve as a crutch for the unprepared speaker.

Humans are the only animal that can communicate to each other an idea of what the future might look like. As far as we know, we are the only animal that can listen to the information another animal provides, and form an image in our mind's eye. We can experience their experiences without actually having been there. We can then heed a very intricate warning about the cause and effect of things. PowerPoint sometimes leads people to reduce complex concepts to ungrammatical bullet points, which on their own don't make any sense. The opposite of this is the speaker who puts everything they're going to say on a slide and then reads it word for word.

Other PowerPoint sins include trying to jam multiple strains of information onto single slides, perhaps using red, yellow and green 'traffic light' systems to indicate threats, identify progress or gauge success. Due to the software's preset layouts, it is common to see distorted, low-resolution images that are intended to support a bullet point message. Worse still is when a topographical map is stretched to fill the slide area, rendering it useless as a planning tool. PowerPoint has a lot to answer for, yet it's overused by so many managers and leaders, inevitably resulting in poor communication.

To my mind, storytelling remains the best, most instinctive way to transmit your information to the minds of others. Creating a memorable story is a great way of reinforcing your point.

In Afghanistan, I sat through PowerPoint presentations that had more than 80 slides. It quickly became apparent to me that these were more an arse-covering exercise and a bureaucratic necessity than a means of sharing information for operational purposes. I would watch the men's eyes glaze over as the target information, the different phases of the plan, the actions and the backup plans were detailed again and again.

Then we would go through the 'rehearsal of concept' (ROC) drill, which would tell a story. Every man would walk through his role, his task, his piece of the puzzle. We were imagining ourselves in the future, and telling the story of events that were yet to unfold.

Later in my life after the Army, I learnt an even more powerful communicative skill: stories within stories. If I had to convey my knowledge about a certain subject, I first had to understand the outcome I was striving for. What did I want to achieve by presenting on this subject? This was the single most important question. Did I want my audience to learn a skill or understand a concept? Or did I want to motivate them to an action? No matter what it was, I needed to understand what the outcome was to be.

From there, I would work out the teaching points I needed to cover to get to that outcome. I would construct each PowerPoint slide around a single teaching aim, and for each slide there would be a story. As this book demonstrates, I have a memory bank full of stories, which I can draw on to illustrate a skill, a philosophical position or a lesson that I've learnt. In my experience, if each Power-Point slide of a presentation is an interactive story to be shared with the group, they are far more likely to absorb the communication as a whole. Our stories really are our best teaching tools.

Of course, not everyone is naturally good at telling stories, but it's something that can be learnt. I've learnt a few tricks to being able to stand up and tell a good story to a crowd of people.

Firstly, you have to capture their attention immediately, and encourage them to visualise themselves as the storyteller. 'I was on my back, covered in dust, looking up to the clear blue sky and wondering how on earth I was going to get out of this one . . .' Or: 'When I was fourteen, I asked Rachel, the girl I sat next to in class, if she'd walk home with me. I was so nervous . . .' In both these examples, the listener can put themselves in the storyteller's place. Chances are they've been in a position that they thought would be hard to get out of, or they've been nervous asking someone on a date. Either way, you have their attention and they feel they can relate to you.

Now it's time to craft the story. It should be descriptive, snappy and authentic, and your delivery needs to be charismatic. There's no point capturing their attention if you can't keep it. I believe that a good start needs to have either a twist or a poignant teaching point, or it needs to have a funny ending. In the military, this is known as 'the arousal'. The arousal is commonly used at the start of a lesson, brief or presentation: it sets the scene, captures the audience's attention and makes them want to come on a journey with you.

There's an art to skilled communication. Developing an understanding of the leader's intent is the key to passing on timely and accurate information. To really master communication, consider storytelling as your medium. Taking people on a narrative journey is a great way to convey your ideas or win someone over to your point of view, rather than just rolling through slides of data.

LESSONS

Communicating effectively to those around you is a skill that takes years to master. It's made harder by those you are trying to communicate to not listening and not observing.

More often than not, a simple message delivered simply is the best way of communicating a concept or idea.

To communicate effectively, you need to choose the correct medium to get your point across, whether it's telling a story, issuing a set of orders or presenting your ideas with an interactive PowerPoint presentation. Don't get locked into delivering the message the wrong way.

Storytelling can be a potent means of engaging an audience and communicating your ideas in a memorable way.

14

THE PERFORMANCE ADVANTAGE MODEL

'We are what we consistently do, excellence then
is not an act but a habit.'

attributed to Aristotle

When I was the Sniper Platoon commander in the Australian Defence Force's Tactical Assault Group–East (TAG East), I developed a concept to drive high performance in both individuals and teams. I call it the Performance Advantage Model, and it looks like this:

$$P = (a + b)c$$

a. *Native Ability*. Your genetic make-up and natural ability.
b. *Training*. Your physical and cognitive development through consistency.
c. *Tribe*. The people who influence your thoughts and actions.

These elements combine to provide a recipe for persistent and non-degrading high performance. I used this formula when developing my yearly training program, and also for the platoon that I deployed to Afghanistan with in 2010. Let me explain it in more detail.

Your native ability is your genetic disposition, and the things that come easy to you are based on this. Some people are just good at certain things, while others find the same skills difficult to master. Perhaps it's ball sports, balance, building muscle, endurance, mathematics, English, retaining information; whatever it is, these native abilities are strengths that support the other aspects of your performance.

Your training can enhance these native abilities. Even working on your weaknesses will help develop your strengths. It's consistent application over time that makes a champion. As the saying goes, 'Hard work beats talent.'

Your natural ability and training both your strengths and your weaknesses will certainly make you a better athlete, soldier and person, but the third aspect is where the magic happens: the people you share your journey with.

Let's look at CrossFit gyms as an example. One of the key reasons for their success is the group training environment—the arduous training has a social aspect. When a fad like paleo eating moves into the CrossFit community, it gains traction. When a new technique is learnt that guarantees better strength or greater efficiency, it is adopted. When young athletes see Masters athletes putting in the hard yards, day after day, they adopt those behaviours too. A community can multiply the combination of natural ability and training.

There has been very little written about the raising of TAG East in 2002, which was a direct response to the 9/11 terrorist attacks that had occurred in the United States the previous year. TAG East is the domestic counter-terrorism response unit based on the east coast of Australia; the response capability is shared with Tactical Assault Group–West (TAG West), which is part of the Special Air Service Regiment (SASR), based in Perth.

I was selected to join the first TAG East training course. To say that the standards were exacting would be a gross understatement. We initially underwent a series of 'environmental' tests at Holsworthy Barracks, before participating in courses and collective training in Perth under the guidance and direction of the SASR, designed to test our capabilities in a range of operating environments. We worked at heights, underwater, in confined spaces and in darkness.

One of my favourite memories was the heights test. We had to wear a gas mask that had been painted so that you could only see a little sliver of light through each lens. We walked up a set of stairs to a beam, made our way along the beam, and then, when instructed, jumped off. I got to the end of the beam and was told to jump, so I squatted down and jumped off.

During the evaluation, I learnt I'd been marked down, and I laughed.

The psychologist in charge of the testing was not amused. 'I don't see how that's funny, Sergeant Connolly. Being afraid of heights means you can't go on with the training.'

I realised it was serious, but I still thought it was funny. 'It's true I'm scared of heights,' I said, watching for a reaction; there was none. 'But if you've done your research, you'll know I'm the lead climber for the unit, having completed a climbing course in the UK, and one here in Australia, and the Mountain Warfare course too.'

I was sure they'd also find this funny, but still there was no reaction.

'Send in the next man,' they told me.

I went out and spent the next few hours sweating on my decision to squat at the end of the beam before jumping off—after all, you have to protect your knees, I told myself.

Nothing more was said about it, though, and soon I found myself in Perth undertaking the TAG training.

Prior to the 9/11 attacks in the United States, Australia's domestic counter-terrorism responsibilities were held exclusively by the SASR. As they were based in Perth, the national capability was hindered by the unit's ability to respond in a timely manner to incidents that occurred on the east coast of Australia. The 1995 Defence White Paper projected that this capability would be based on the east coast by 2005, but this was expedited after the 9/11 attacks. The SASR was never going to move from Perth, so a decision was made to stand up TAG East from my unit, 4RAR (Commando), now the 2nd Commando Regiment. This required the SASR to simultaneously man a TAG on the east coast, deploy a squadron to Afghanistan, and train members of my unit to be the new TAG East. They liked to call us the baby TAG.

I know the training we did was legitimate. The SASR didn't want us there, and made it very hard for us. We spent the mornings running, then were on the range shooting, and in the afternoons learnt movement tactics. The glide path over the initial four-week course went from individual skills, then multi-person skills, then team skills, then multiple teams in a single room, then multiple teams in multiple rooms, then multi-team, multi-room and multi-level all at once. The pace was frantic.

Weaknesses were exposed and individuals were weeded out. Those with natural pistol shooting abilities excelled, as pistol shooting was the primary requirement to move forward. I've always been good with a long gun, but the short-barrel weapons were foreign to me. I was in the instructor's sights when I failed to validate with the ageing Browning Hi-Power 9-millimetre pistol. I struggled for a few days before the training paid off. The people around me who were passing were confident, and when I started to pass I became confident too.

We ate together, ran together, trained together, and drank together on the weekends. We completed the basic close-quarter battle course together, rolled into the advanced course, then the build-up training, which involved advanced individual skills such as sniping, fast tactical driving and using explosives to effect building entry. I went away and did the sniper course, then the sniper instructor course, the helicopter marksmanship course, and the close-quarter battle instructor course too. Then we came together as one entity.

For the next four years we sat up at Luscombe Airfield as TAG East. On paper we were C Company of 4RAR (Commando), but in reality we were a separate entity. We relied on our parent unit for manpower but operated quite separately due to the day-to-day work location and the roles and tasks it focused on. There was a trickle system for manning into TAG East, and that remained largely unchanged for half a decade.

It could be said that over its first five or six years, the Australian TAG East was the best in the world. We started imparting knowledge back to the SASR, as they had been focusing on operations in the Middle Eastern Area of Operations. This was because of our native abilities and our consistent training, reinforced by the fact that our tribe was intact. We'd experienced very little change over time, apart from our growth and development.

Both the west and east coast TAGs are still considered world-class, and the Performance Advantage Model describes how they became that way. Our native ability and training, multiplied by an exacting culture of excellence, produced sustained high performance.

With various companies rotating through the TAG East responsibility since that time, some of the knowledge continuum and the effects of all being together in that high-performance training environment have been diminished. While rotations exposed a greater number of personnel to the capability, and so lifted the overall effectiveness of the unit, it could also be argued that it caused organisational momentum to be lost.

Another great example of the Performance Advantage Model working well is the Australian cricket team. Each player is selected for his natural abilities or strengths; after all, cricket is a team game played by individuals. When a batsman is at the crease, it's him versus the bowler, then it's him versus the fielders and then him as part of a partnership. Training focuses first on the individual, then on the team, and finally on the other team and how to exploit their individual or team weaknesses.

The secret sauce is the tribe, the character of those who make up the team. The longer they're together, the more successful they should become. In this way, team strengths mitigate individual weaknesses.

It also stands to reason that the leader is the critical piece of the puzzle. A high-performing leader drives subordinates to create a high-performing culture. The result of a high performing culture is obviously high performance. Let's say that leadership is centred around providing clarity of purpose through motivation and direction. The high-performing leader provides the road map to the team, identifying obstacles and illuminating upcoming opportunities. They keep the team focused on maintaining a culture of excellence. Culture then, is about people with shared values and norms of behaviour, a tribe, who often share the same habits so when one excels the whole team seeks to excel. Performance is about getting shit done. It's about the outputs or the outcomes required for mission success.

The test of this concept is when you replace individuals in key positions, or a few people in the tribe. If the tribe remains successful, you've got the formula right. The next big test is rotating a larger number of people into the tribe, or even replacing the whole tribe at once. This is much harder to do, but if your people, your training and processes are good, and if you have a good tribal culture, you can achieve it.

LESSONS

Ability plus training multiplied by culture equals a consistently high-performing team. To put it another way, training the right people in the right way in the right environment builds a healthy and successful organisation.

The high-performing leader drives a high-performing culture which drives high performance.

15

SLEEP IS A WEAPON

'Sleep is the number one recovery and performance
enhancement and guess what, it's free!'

Dr Ian Duncan PhD

There are two critical elements to rejuvenation: sleep and reset. If
you don't get enough sleep, it is detrimental to your health. If you
don't conduct a reset, you will not be able to maintain high performance over your lifetime. I see people worrying about all sorts of
things. They worry about their diets, they worry about their training
regime, they worry about cutting back on coffee or cutting back on
alcohol. There are people who count their macros, adjusting their
schedules to work out harder or longer, or lowering their workouts
because they think they're burnt out. Yet they never ever worry
about their sleep. Sleep is the most important ingredient in any
training program.

It's been said that you can sleep when you're dead, but in fact
you'll be dead a lot sooner if you're not getting the right amount of
sleep in a 24-hour period as often as possible. You have to sleep to
win, sleep to perform and sleep to recover. Sleep is a weapon and you
should rearm yourself often.

The truth is that I've always loved sleep, and I've long realised
the benefits of it—from anti-ageing to mental and physical performance. And I'm not alone in understanding this—there's a mountain
of studies on sleep and its advantages. This might all seem like

common sense, but the truth is we live in a sleep-deprived society. In my opinion, much of what goes wrong with the world has to do with chronic sleep deprivation over a long period of time.

Many of us are time-poor and have multiple projects on the go. We're ambitious or we're trying to be everything to everyone, or perhaps it's the impact of our families and our desire to 'have it all'. Well, you can't have it all, and often we forgo sleep in an effort to extend our productive hours every day. But when you start eating into your sleep time to be more productive, everything you do is inevitably of a lower quality.

When I was younger, I would put myself to bed at around 8.30 pm and get up at 6 am—this was my habit from as far back as I can remember, all through primary school and high school. I still sleep about eight hours a night these days, and if I could, I would extend this even further. I'm not saying that everyone needs the same amount of sleep; I'm well aware that sleep patterns and length are specific to each individual.

However, if you want to do just one thing that will profoundly change your life, then I suggest blocking out time for sleep as well as time for training in every 24-hour period. For me, sleep occurs between 9 pm and 5 am, and physical training is set for between 5 am and 6 am. Anything else I can get is an added extra. And I don't start getting to bed at 9 pm either—that's time to be in the sack and pumping out the zzzs.

Let me tell you about real sleep deprivation and what it does to you. Most of you have been awake all night and have then gone to work the next day—you know that feels terrible—but that's not what I'm talking about. In the Army we often did that. We might have a guard duty all day and all night, and then back it up with a full work day. While it's not optimal, you can get through it and then have a great sleep the next night. What I'm talking about is having to be awake for 48 to 72 hours—or longer.

In Afghanistan in 2008, I was the operations officer (OPSO) for the Commando Company Group (CCG) as part of the Special Operations Task Group (SOTG). Invariably I would pull all-night shifts during critical incidents, and then back up the next day to cover shifts so that the watchkeepers could catch up on their sleep. This went on for months, until I was required to deploy with the CCG outside the wire due to an injury to the company sergeant major.

If I thought that I was enduring sleep deprivation as the OPSO, I was soon re-educated. The tour was close to seven months by the time we landed back in Australia. On returning home, I realised that I was a mess—and the reason was all the sleep deprivation I had endured. It had been a cumulative misery and was impacting every other area of my life. It took me months to be able to sleep soundly at night and experience deep sleep again. More than this, my mind was racing because of the work I'd been doing: I'd always been on call, ready to respond to a critical incident. This would be easy to misdiagnose as post-traumatic stress disorder when in fact I was just burnt out. I needed to reset.

———

What I had discovered was that I needed to have a reset countdown going in the background at all times. For me, the importance of going 'off the grid' and resetting my mind and soul couldn't be understated. Let me explain.

I'm sure most people who know me consider me an extrovert, but those who know me well will agree that I'm actually an introvert. A task-focused introvert! I have about a 30-minute attention span for caring about others' opinions or entertaining their thoughts, and then I need to find an exit. It took me 30 years to work this out about myself, and I left a trail of destruction behind me. (At least, that's how it feels to an introvert who is trying to be an extrovert . . .)

I enjoy the company of others, but I like to think my own thoughts and ponder things; if you tell me something cool, I don't want to keep talking to you, I want to go off and think about it—a lot! My mind is usually racing all day after a conversation.

The world we live in is insanely fast-paced, and nearly everyone is interconnected. Between the invasiveness of social media, the demand to instantly respond to messaging and the constant requirement to be available and on call to your boss, there's no let-up. People often tell me they feel like they're drowning in work, and then when they do have a break it's stressful, as it's still interrupted by emails and work.

I'm a massive believer in scheduling breaks. And I don't mean a weekend in Bali, but meaningful, soul-searching, life-defining breaks. The sort of adventures that involve planning, risk and reward, and the hope of just making it out alive.

Our personalities usually dictate what sort of break we want. A relaxing break where you lie by the pool with a good book is fine for some people, but I need adventure, the unknown and self-discovery. It might sound strange, but relaxing and being absolutely smashed can both serve as a reset. If you need to relax, so be it. And if you need to be exhausted and challenged by the end of your break, that's just as good.

Some people have professions or jobs that are so mentally taxing that for them to reset, they need not only to go off the grid, but also to immerse themselves in nothing—to stop thinking and just exist for a while. Others have jobs that are so mind-numbing that they'll want to be challenged, stretched mentally and physically so they can leave their reset with a newfound resilience.

So how do we plan a meaningful reset? Well, it has to be epic, and far enough along in the calendar that it requires not only planning, but also a series of steps, either training or preparation. Then—and this is the trick—you must set the date.

Once you've committed to a date, it's a matter of understanding what you want to achieve from the reset. What is it about this break that is going to drive you and maintain your motivation on those long, crappy workdays? I like to plan my break like a future mission. I choose a D-day, and then work my way back so that I understand the gross training requirements that will get me to the starting point.

One of the resets I am undertaking this year is to race another triathlon in Dubai. I'm also using the reset to stop thinking about (most of) my multiple projects for a week, and to focus on writing this book. The race will demand a certain amount of physical training preparation, while the book will also require me to set some conditions so I'm successful in the limited time I'll have. The race is going to be arduous (a half-ironman) and the training in the final four weeks will be the most challenging aspect.

It's not the perfect reset for me; it's something of a compromise. A perfect reset would be disappearing into the Australian bush. Probably the coastal areas of the north-west, where I'd hunt and fish by myself for a month.

When I returned from my second tour to Afghanistan, I took four weeks off. I purchased a four-wheel drive trailer, a BMW G450X motorbike, and all the camping and fishing gear. I drove from Melbourne to Adelaide, and then on to Balgowan, on the Yorke Peninsula in South Australia. I set up camp there and rode my bike all over the peninsula, exploring tracks and dunes and hidden fishing spots.

I loved every minute of it. I was in charge of me. I would hunt for food or go hungry, or sometimes go to a small local store and buy what I needed. I spent some days walking for kilometres, leaving my bike hidden in the scrub, and then come back at nightfall and either sleep there or ride back to my camp.

Getting the right amount of sleep and conducting a reset enables you to perform optimally. Not just for a day, a week, a month or a year, but for a lifetime. Taking time to rejuvenate your body and your mind will yield positive results, and you'll draw upon these in the future. Once you decide to make proper sleep and regular resets a part of your life, your only challenge is to have the discipline to maintain it.

What's my next life reset going to be? I think that once this book finally hits the bookshelves I'll walk the Camino de Santiago in Spain—the whole damn thing!

LESSONS

Sleep is a weapon. Rearm often.

Regular and consistent deep sleep is a key habit you need to develop to be successful. You might get by for periods without the correct amount, or even without any sleep at all, but the cost comes later.

Just as important is the reset. This can take many forms, and depends on your personality, life situation and needs. But the idea is to get away from your day-to-day experience of life and reset your mind and body, allowing them to prepare for the challenges ahead.

16

BUILD SITUATIONAL AWARENESS

'There are things known, and there are things unknown,
and in between are the doors of perception.'

attributed to Aldous Huxley

Good situational awareness—physical, emotional and social—is vital for an operator in the Special Forces, allowing them to predict outcomes more accurately. If the average person develops this skill to a high standard, it can be a force multiplier, increasing their achievements exponentially.

A person has situational awareness when they are in tune both with the environment around them and with the behaviours of the people or things interacting within that environment. To have situational awareness, a person must first be aware that there are cues, and then be able to observe and interpret these cues. If they can understand the meaning of the cues, they're in a better position to make a prediction about what will happen next.

The cues are the foundation on which situational awareness is based, and there are many types: topographical information, or streetscape, or room layout; the position of objects, dead spaces, heights and depths, and hidden areas; climatic effects associated with the environment; the movement of objects and their speed in relation to other objects; the behavioural actions of individuals or groups; equipment and operating systems and the stimulus they represent (radios, dashboards, computers and so on).

Observing these cues is just the start. To be situationally aware, a person must understand the cues—and the depth of their understanding will inform to the depth of their situational awareness.

Generally, knowledge of what each cue represents is gained primarily through exposure and experience. This can be enhanced through formal education or training. Further depth is gained through shared normative behaviours and beliefs, symbols and procedures—better known as culture. This might occur in the form of storytelling or conversation.

For instance, a young child has no idea how dangerous a road is. For an adult, the dangers are obvious. An adult approaches the road with a heightened degree of situational awareness. They can discern different types of traffic noises (cars, buses, trams, trains), they understand vehicle movement speeds and driver behaviours, as well as the many non-verbal signals used in the environment: lights, horns, bells and so on. All of these shape the person's situational awareness, and allow them to make a reliable estimation about what will happen next.

Most adults have the added advantage of having done formal driver training—perhaps even extra road safety training or job-specific driving training as well, depending on their employment. In addition, they've heard stories about traffic accidents, perhaps even seen some first-hand, and watched news reports about fatalities. The cues they've learnt have been reinforced, and the stories and training validated. In this way, it's clear, most adults have heightened situational awareness around roads.

Here's another example, this one from my time with TAG East. The operators within the TAG conduct physical training not unlike Olympic athletes, and the tactical training for their kinetic response is world-class. They take their role very seriously, and an important requirement of each operator is the ability to demonstrate constant situational awareness.

On the initial training course for the TAG, known as the close-quarter battle course, an operator is required to demonstrate an ability to differentiate between people, targets, friends and foe, hostages and terrorists. This occurs in increasingly demanding environments and increasingly complex situations. I can't go into specifics about this, but suffice it to say that our key advantage, as an assault force against any enemy of Australia, is that our personnel have been selected and trained to ensure they have all the attributes, including situational awareness.

Eight years after I was first 'on team' with TAG East, there I was, in the dark, standing outside a green metal double-door. It was not more than an hour before dawn, and as dark as a night can get with the moon already set. The rest of my platoon were outside various other doors, or on ladders, peeking over walls, or on roofs, scanning courtyards. Some were in blocking positions; all were ready. The Death Head lot (Delta Company) were in place.

A drone circled overhead. The pilot, who could well have been back in Arizona, gave me continuous feedback on who was moving where: some were threats and others were friendlies, or blue force. The wind was warm, evidence of the sweltering day before, and the smell of human waste was strong, highlighting my proximity to the enemy's latrine, at the east of the compound.

I smiled. My night-vision goggles turned night into day, but they limited my vision, reducing my situational awareness to only a small circle outlined by darkness. My other senses were heightened as a result.

In my mind's eye I knew where the other entry teams were, and the teams' radio calls confirmed our rehearsals. I knew the compounds like the back of my hand—I could have built them, I knew them so well. I looked down at my watch, bringing it up to the left monocular, which was specifically set to read the time at close range.

The seconds ticked by. There was no need for a radio call; the synchronisation of our watches and the absence of an abort command from me or my team leaders reinforced that the plan was going ahead.

I felt a squeeze on my right shoulder, and I in turn squeezed the shoulder of the man in front. Five seconds later an explosion disintegrated the green metal doors, and in an instant we were sprinting into the dust. Smoke had filled the room, and debris fell. I cleared the fatal funnel of the doorway and was into the room, my safety catch off, weapon up, laser on.

Shooting started from my right and in the rooms ahead of me, outside and all around. Sparks flew as grenades ruptured the air. Bullets, in pairs, ricocheted off walls, zipping past my head and over my shoulder and across my chest. I knew our weapons by the unmistakable sound of their suppressors, then a larger weapon came to life, then another, and another still, but all stopped as abruptly as they'd started. Finally this first room was clear.

My team and I moved into a courtyard. After this there were more rooms to clear—all were in my primary area of responsibility. We were like land sharks, chomping and biting and doing everything sharks do when they go into a feeding frenzy.

To everything else, a shark in a frenzy looks like it's out of control—it's tearing, biting, thrashing and smashing its prey. But another shark will see this as controlled aggression, business as usual. I knew the sharks behind me and in front of me, and I understood what they were doing. Small cues continually fed into my mental computer, ever updating, allowing me to make sense of the situation.

Suddenly a target registered to my front, and it met all the requirements to be neutralised—fuck it, *eliminated*. In mid-stride I snatched at my trigger, then cursed myself for my enthusiasm. I slowed my breathing and gently manipulated the trigger again; it jumped in my hands and the bolt held back, I knew what it was without even looking to see the fault, as I'd felt it a thousand times before.

Before I even consciously processed what I was doing, I dropped the M4 out of my hands, the three-point sling taking its weight. In a less confined space, I would have carried out the immediate action (IA) drill, but not here, not now. The target was still available—he'd taken exception to being shot and could kill me in a moment.

Instantly my Heckler & Koch USP pistol was out, up in front of my line of sight and barking in my hands, then it was back away and I was down on a knee, inserting a new magazine into my M4. A teammate fired over my head, finally putting the problem to bed.

This was situational awareness training in practice. The location was the Afghan Village at Holsworthy Barracks, in south-western Sydney, and the same assault was carried out hundreds of times to supplement our counter-terrorist training and prepare us for our role in Afghanistan the following year. All manner of permutations were considered, and all scenarios played out. These ranged from the benign to the unimaginable—but we not only imagined the unimaginable, we rehearsed killing it or controlling it too.

Nine months later, my compete platoon from TAG East were in Afghanistan. We conducted a helicopter insertion, dropping just outside a huge compound. Outnumbered and seriously outgunned, we were pinned down as soon as we landed.

Enemy fighters suppressed our movement and separated my force. We fought for our lives, and three teams, including mine, finally broke into the enemy's fortress. We had no other choice than to go to where land sharks were comfortable: inside complexity. The enemy used women and children as shields and hostages; they fired machine guns at us from close range and threw grenades from room to room. They were panicked and confused and fired at ghosts. We prevailed, with no loss either to my force or to the besieged civilians.

Once we were inside the buildings, it was a violent and fast-paced fight. For me, it was confirmation of our nation's ability to respond to enemies on home soil, should it ever be needed.

I can't emphasise enough that our most fearsome weapon is situational awareness; that is, being at one with your environment. An operator understands the absence of normality or the presence of an abnormality. These two things are critical indicators of something not being right. If a village market is usually busy, thriving with people trading goods, and then all of a sudden it starts emptying out and becomes like a ghost town this would be an indicator of an absence of normality. Whenever we saw this in Afghanistan it was highly likely the shooting was about to start. Conversely, if we saw a couple of people milling around a corner watching our movements and trying to look natural, this could mean the presence of an abnormality. The absence of normality or the presence of an abnormality are the best indicators of something happening in your environment that you are not in control of or something happening in your environment that you may need to react to.

Having good situational awareness isn't just a brilliant survival mechanism, it also means you can predict what will occur next and prepare to respond with no delay, allowing you to shape the world around you. There is no more powerful tool.

LESSONS

Situational awareness can be built over time by looking for environmental cues that provide feedback on how an activity is progressing.

Temper your situational awareness with knowledge of your thinking biases. Do not allow yourself to be sucked into making poor decisions based on incorrect assumptions.

Working in a team environment for extended periods builds better knowledge of how those around you will act, allowing you to make better decisions in the moment.

A team's eyes and ears become your eyes and ears, providing you with constant feedback of how your adversary is reacting to your actions.

A main indicator of pending danger is the absence of normality or the presence of an abnormality.

17

INVEST IN PEOPLE

'Those that you teach will also become your teachers—
everyone is on a journey of development.'

Rabia Siddique

The human mind is the greatest untapped resource on the planet, and as a leader you should invest time and effort into making best use of it—your mind and the minds of the people you lead. If you are selfless in developing others, it will increase your effectiveness many times over.

I looked at the document sitting on my desk, and felt embarrassment flood over me. Glancing over my shoulder, I saw that the major's door was open, and for a moment I considered walking down the hallway and going in there to apologise. I thought better of it, though, and sank into my chair to look over the operations order that had reappeared on my desk.

It was 2005, and I had recently moved positions, leaving my role as senior sniper and tactical planner within TAG East, and becoming the operations sergeant. I'd been successful in my application to become an officer a few months earlier, and because of this I was set to transfer from the enlisted rank of sergeant to a Queen's commission rank of captain. At the end of the year I would be posted to the 1st Commando Company as their brand-new operations officer, and it had been decided that serving as operations sergeant would help set me up for success in that positing.

My boss, the officer in charge (or OC) of the company, had asked me to construct an operations order to move the TAG out to Garden Island, in Sydney Harbour, where we'd conduct a series of rehearsals and then a full mission profile. The operation would involve multiple assets, including boats, helicopters and a naval ship, all operating together over the course of a week. The New South Wales Police Force were also involved, as were some other supporting agencies.

This type of training requires a lot of informal and formal conversations, and a high degree of project management skill. I'd been working with the operations officer, and had attended all the meetings with him. The plan was set in stone and the working parts had all been agreed to, with everyone notified. It had all come together nicely, due in part to our good planning and the energy that we had injected into the process. I had multiple whiteboards full of dates and times, capturing the mechanics of the week ahead.

The final thing needed to ensure the training went off without a hitch was to formally lock everything in place and synchronise the efforts of the Army and Navy. To do this, the TAG uses operations orders rather than training directives or exercise directives or a loose training plan; in this way we train like we fight. The process is formal, structured and can be used to present to government. It's the same process we use if we're on real operations in another country.

The OC had asked me on Thursday the week prior to write the order, and he'd given me a deadline of a few weeks. I'd spent two days behind the computer writing it up, and had dropped it on his desk at 4 pm on the Friday, before taking an early mark and going home. I spent the weekend in Cronulla—we refer to it as God's country—running, kayaking, kite surfing and drinking. Now it was Monday morning.

I'd finished my physical training for the day and was at my desk at 9 am. In front of me was the document. There was more red pen across the pages than typeset black ink: every page had note flags, and under the printout was a book, also tagged. I knew the book instantly: it was the *Australian Defence Force Publication 102*—the writing standards of the ADF.

My heart sank. The boss had returned from a meeting on the Friday afternoon to find my drivel sitting on his desk. I visualised him sitting there, flicking through the pages and shaking his head. I knew his work ethic well, and imagined him sitting there well past midnight, red-penning the sentences. For every red mark there was a referral to the *ADFP 102*. In some cases, he had also written explanations of why we write things the way we do.

While I was flicking through the document, the OC came out of his office and walked down the hallway. He said good morning to me as he passed my desk, but he did not refer to the document. I was still sitting there looking at the pages when he returned a few hours later. I didn't notice him come in, but I did notice the message that popped up on my computer to bring the operations order to his office. I rose and sheepishly went down the hallway to the OC's office.

Sitting next to me at his round conference table, he took me through the document, line by line and page by page, referring to the *ADFP 102* and explaining the mistakes I'd made. He was never once flustered, angry or even dismissive of me. In fact, the OC was the model of patience. I'm embarrassed to say I was frustrated by the experience, and even bored in some ways. My attention span was short, and I was finding it hard to concentrate. But he persisted.

When we were done, I returned to my desk, and then I spent the whole week rewriting the operations order. Line by line, I checked what I was writing and made sure that it adhered to the conventions outlined in the style guide. I double-checked my work; it was my goal not to see any red pen on the next version. When Friday came, I put the finished document on the OC's desk at 5 pm and went home.

When I returned to work on Monday morning, I had to fight the impulse to go straight to my desk to see if the OC had returned the operations order. I went for a long run on the track behind Luscombe Airfield, up Heartbreak Hill and along the top of the escarpment to the turnaround point and back—a 10-kilometre run, and a favourite of the lads back in the day. Then it was back to the Grots (large lockers specifically made for TAG members) for a shower. I put my flight suit on and had breakfast. At 9 am I sat down at my desk.

There, waiting for me, was the document—covered in pen corrections and note flags. This time, though, the mark-up was in blue, not red, and the notes referenced all manner of Australian Defence Force documents, none of which was the *ADFP 102*.

I quickly saw that the OC had invested more time in my development—this time focusing on how to frame the orders, and the way the other organisations needed to be compelled to do what the document was designed to get them to do. There were redundancies built into the document, second-order effects, actions on, timings and forecast requirements. The document had been transformed from a list of roles and tasks to a piece of leadership art that would make the activity work. Once again, I was humbled.

Later that day, when we sat down to discuss the changes, the OC told me he had decided to use blue pen so his criticism wouldn't be seen as negative, and so that he might keep my attention longer. This wasn't intended as an insult, and I didn't take it that way—and it worked. I understood that he was on a journey too.

I returned to my desk and threw my intellect into the document once again. I researched other strategic documents, and I rang stakeholders and discussed their roles. In short, I became an operations officer. By the end of that week I had completed the final document, which was due to be issued to the participants the following Monday. I walked it into the OC's office and we went through it one final time. We checked all the references, line by line, until he was satisfied that it was complete. Three days later we released my first operational order to the stakeholders and participants.

Over the next six months I wrote another eight operational orders for TAG East. The OC checked the first few, and after that he was confident enough in me to release them with his signature after only a cursory glance.

There's a quote as old as time itself: 'Give a man a fish and you feed him for a day; teach a man to fish and you feed him for a lifetime.' The OC had taught me to fish, and by investing in my development in that way, he had built a trusted and reliable staff officer on whom he could depend to capture his intent and expedite the process of writing and issuing his orders.

This was one of the most profound experiences of my military career. I had been a cocky young man, especially when, as a sergeant, I was successful in my application to become an officer. The selection board had seen something in me but I had yet to see it in myself. I had no right to act cocky at all. I hadn't been to the Royal Military College; really, I needed to show a lot more humility, and demonstrate a thirst for knowledge. I cringe at the thought of becoming an officer without having had this humbling experience.

In the years that followed, I made it my mission to produce the highest-quality documents, always striving to avoid any trace of a senior officer's red pen. And that was a tough challenge, because they all had their idiosyncrasies. The Commanding Officer (CO) of the Special Forces Training Centre was my hardest taskmaster. Under his guidance, I rewrote the official document for the Special Forces Direct Entry Scheme, revitalising the scheme; I was awarded a Special Operations Commander Australia Commendation for my efforts. This was from Major General Mike Hindmarsh, an officer for whom I had the highest respect. Receiving that commendation is still one of my proudest moments.

I did my best to invest in the same way in my own subordinates. I only ever corrected their work in blue pen, and I took the time to flag and reference any changes that I made. I wanted my subordinates to feel the same genuine concern for their professional development that had been shown to me by the OC of TAG East and then the CO of the Special Forces Training Centre. In fact, this investment in my subordinates became more important to me than most other things. It certainly made me a much more effective leader.

LESSONS

Don't just correct someone when you can use the moment to teach them something.

Professional development happens when you take longer to complete a task by involving a subordinate, with the aim of teaching them how to do something to a high standard in the future.

When you truly appreciate the power of investing in your people's knowledge, understanding and abilities, you will always take the time and opportunity to improve them.

LEADERSHIP

18

DEFINING LEADERSHIP

'Leadership is the art of getting someone else to do
something you want done because he wants to do it.'

President Dwight D. Eisenhower

There's a big difference between management and leadership, and yet people often confuse the two. During my years in the Army, I regularly asked friends to define leadership. What I learnt was that most of us can't put our finger on a definition—and that not only is leadership hard to define, it's also difficult to conceptualise. Most people see leadership as getting other people to do things they don't want to do. This isn't a bad crack at a definition, but it has a way to go.

Another thing I learnt over the years is that leadership is often done badly. It's a skill that is regularly misunderstood, and in some cases abused. When thinking about leadership, our minds too easily picture someone in a position of power being forceful and showing disregard for their subordinates or followers.

Many leaders assume their roles and daily actions should revolve around keeping work harmonious and making sure subordinates are happy and motivated. The day I worked out that the opposite was true was the day I actually became a leader. Prior to then I had been just a benevolent peace keeper.

Ever since my first leadership role, I have wanted to understand what leadership really was. To uncover a true definition of leadership, and to see how it works in practice, I had to break the concept down into its component parts, study them and then reassemble them. I wanted to understand the essence of leadership, and to do that I first had to deal with the elephant in the room: management.

Management is simply a business or administrative function. It exists to deliver services or to ensure that a process is adhered to. The difference between a manager and a leader is stark—and it should be. There are leaders who may need to manage as part of their jobs, and there are managers who may need to lead in order to be effective, but we should never mistake one for the other. A manager is concerned with supporting business processes, while a leader focuses on human performance. They can be mutually supporting skills, or they can be concerned with one or other aspect exclusively.

The definition of leadership that I adhere to has been articulated well by Simon Sinek and immortalised in pop culture: 'Leadership is getting others to do what you want them to do because they want to do it.' The way to achieve this is through influence, which helps you build trust. Trust has to go both ways, and there's no fast road to achieving it.

The Army teaches that there are three theoretical styles of leadership: directive, participative and delegative. A good leader is able to transcend these, using one or all of them as required by the situational context or the nature of their subordinates.

A directive style is appropriate when the leader must demonstrate specific expectations, such as when teaching someone a specific skill. It's also used when a leader wants to reinforce a certain standard, or in an emergency or crisis where there are time constraints.

A participative style is appropriate when the team has a good understanding of their roles and tasks, when the leader wants to build team cohesion through shared experiences, when a leader wants to be seen leading from the front, or when a leader wants to build rapport with their subordinates.

Delegative leadership is considered the holy grail of leadership. It's used when the leader trusts their subordinates to completely understand how a task is to be done, when the leader is in charge of a high-performing team and trusts that the subordinates will self-motivate and deliver the expected outputs, or when a leader's subordinates are also good leaders who are capable of applying the various leadership styles as the context requires.

When we pull apart the various leadership styles, we can see certain themes and words jumping out. Participative leadership focuses on expectations and standards, as well as time management. Participative leadership emphasises team cohesion through demonstration and shared experiences. Delegative leadership has trust at its core.

And it's also clear that if delegative leadership is the gold standard, the two other styles encourage the building of trust. This suggests that time is a hidden but very important aspect of leadership.

There is one other hidden component at play here, and it's probably the hardest to articulate: influence. It's there in each of the leadership styles, but becomes more significant as we move towards delegative leadership. Your aim should be to build *influence* with a subordinate, so that *trust* develops—and this takes *time*.

Influencing a subordinate means using your experiences, education or frames of reference to support the reasons why you want a task done a certain way. If you don't do this, they'll find their own way—and their trust in you will be eroded.

———

In peacetime, I'm not sure that many of the leaders I encountered in the Army were particularly good at leadership as defined by Sinek. The best leadership lessons I experienced came the hard way, while I was in combat.

The junior non-commissioned officer courses don't go into anywhere near enough detail about the theory of leadership and how to lead your peers, which is what a lance corporal or corporal actually has to do. The sergeant career courses touched on the theory, but most of the lessons focused on professionalism and technical competency. We learnt to lead through administration, and of course from mentoring by the platoon commander.

The warrant officer courses were brilliant, though, and the lessons were transferable in some ways to my role as an officer, too. Having said that, most of the guys I attended these courses with were some years older than me and had an eye on getting out in a few years—or, worse still, they were there simply because of their time in that rank, and they had no real aspirations to be a leader.

The officers themselves were okay leaders, but they were often one-dimensional in their style. Leading through example, the cookie-cutter version of leadership, seemed to be their default setting.

Of course, I was an officer who came through the ranks, so I'm not qualified to talk about what other officers learnt at the Australian Defence Force Academy or the Royal Military College. The leadership theory they were taught was probably very good. Yet my platoon commanders were never all that good at getting us to do what they wanted us to do *because* we wanted to do it. They generally just told us to do stuff, and then demonstrated how they were doing it with us, down in the trenches. One notable exception was Vince Creagh, my platoon commander in Somalia in 1993 and his leadership seemed to change only when we went to war. Combat operations change the dynamic completely.

The commanders I had on operations took a completely different approach to leadership. They were able to get us wanting to do what we had to. No doubt group survival was a major motivation: they could appeal to our need to survive this threat to our lives together.

Why does combat bring out the best in a leader? Well, when a threat is real, and not just perceived, leaders often discover and harness another key aspect of leadership: energy transference.

One thing leaders aren't formally taught is that in order to gain any traction while in command, you have to bring huge amounts of energy. Leadership is complex, but at its core it is energy transference. And there are a few ways to harness this energy transference as the next chapter shows.

LESSONS

Leadership is making others want to do what you need them to do. It requires influence, trust and time.

Leadership and management are not the same. Management requires little interaction or influence; leadership relies upon successful interaction and influence.

There are three leadership styles: directive, participative and delegative. Leaders should be proficient in all three styles, even if they're stronger in one and weaker in another.

Leading by example becomes increasingly difficult and less effective as the size of a group increases. As you rise up the chain of command and your organisation gets bigger, you can't be as participative, but you must remain positively connected to the individuals you lead.

Successful leaders appeal to their subordinates' sense of ownership of a shared problem.

19

THE ELEVEN PRINCIPLES OF LEADERSHIP

'A high performing team is the product of a high performing
culture, which is in turn a product of high performing leaders.'

Brian Elloy

In the military, we use a lot of acronyms. There are two main purposes: to shorten a long-winded name, concept or object, or to help us remember lists. A great example of the latter is the eleven principles of leadership—Courage, Motivation, Decisiveness, Responsibility, Selflessness, Integrity, Loyalty, Initiative, Judgement, Ability to communicate, and Knowledge—which I recall as CMDR SILI JAK, or 'Commander Silly Jack'. Let's take a look at each in turn.

Courage is a virtue associated with heroes performing brave deeds, and this will always be so. As a leadership principle, it's different. There is no reason why leaders can't perform brave deeds, but if they're being brave only in the face of danger and not in front of the people they're leading, something has gone wrong. Leaders are frequently asked to do things they may not agree with or want to undertake. Some leaders will follow a higher direction without question, as they may not want to incur the wrath of their superiors. Good leaders, though, will show courage and wisely challenge directions, orders and guidance. Strong leaders have the best interests of their subordinates in mind. They are also courageous in their decision-making, and do not take the easy option when dealing with subordinates.

Motivation in a good leader has two forms: self-motivation and group motivation. Self-motivation is what keeps a leader going in both good times and bad. At a basic level, this means keeping physically and mentally fit, having a routine that gets them out of bed early and at work on time, and projecting an image that their peers, superiors and subordinates respect. Leaders strive to accomplish a long-term result, not just a short-term performance. They do this to maintain a positive outlook that keeps them focused on developing the organisation in their charge, so they can eventually pass on a group that has sustained or improved its capabilities. The example set by such a leader has the effect of motivating those around them do achieve and eventually surpass the standards that have been set. Leaders are mindful of bringing their organisation along with them, and making every member feel a part of the team. But after all this is said and done, please remember this: motivation lights the fire, consistency builds an inferno.

Decisiveness is a quality that any good leader must have; if they don't have it, they're in the wrong business. To enable good decisions to be made, leaders must consider all the facts and knowledge at their disposal. This does not mean they must come up with every answer themselves; they rely upon their team to offer expertise, knowledge and possible solutions. Once the leader has all the inputs, they are now in a position to make a decision—but time can also be a factor. Frequently a leader must make a decision without the opportunity for the consultation they are accustomed to; this means taking a risk. A good leader mentors and develops subordinates, involving them in the decision-making process. This develops a team mentality, which can shrink the organisational decision-making loop, making it more efficient. The team should have confidence that their leader will make a decision with their best interests at heart, and the leader should be confident in the team's abilities and trust.

Responsibility is part of the job of a leader, and must be practised. Human nature pushes us to avoid it, but we must accept it in order to grow as a person. If we're to learn from our mistakes, we must first recognise we have made a mistake. It is easier to blame another, but a good friend, a trusted mentor or a respected subordinate can provide clarity when we mess up; we must treat it as an opportunity for self-reflection. Responsibility for the wellbeing of an organisation is also something the leader must accept, as it drives our motivations and the decision-making process. A leader must be responsible for the actions of the group, and own the outcome, whether it is desirable or not. A consequence of taking responsibility for a group is to allow subordinates the freedom to make mistakes, to help them fix those mistakes, and then to own any possible fallout. This is hard to practise in an operational environment, for obvious reasons, but with discipline it can be practised in training. In this way a leader becomes responsible for the development of the organisation, and the successes and mistakes made along the way.

Selflessness, at a basic level, refers to the concept of going without so that another person does not miss out. This is the opposite of what we might instinctively do in a survival situation, but comes naturally when we feel responsible for the health, wellbeing and benefit of another person. Parents go without so that their children do not, and as the children mature, they come to appreciate this, and will enact it themselves when they have children. As parents, we make sacrifices to ensure our children succeed, and leading a group or organisation is much the same. Leaders must show selflessness in order to build trust. In the military, leaders make a point of eating, drinking or receiving a benefit last; the lesson is that they will always look after the group ahead of themselves, and this increases the commitment of the group. The leader, in turn, is motivated by the knowledge that when the entire group is being looked after well, he or she will benefit as well. A good leader often sacrifices time to management and planning tasks, which sees them working longer hours than those they command. This can take a toll, but a good leadership team will ensure that a commander's efforts to be selfless do not result in him or her suffering.

Integrity is a value we all look for in everyone we meet, but especially leaders. The leader achieves integrity by being accountable at all times. In the first place, an individual must be true to the standards they expect their group to uphold, whether these are physical, technical or ethical. At the organisational level, a leader must be truthful. He or she must strive to keep the group appropriately informed at all times. When information is of a 'need to know' nature, a good leader is clear about this, and might explain the reasons for this and promote an understanding that this is an operational requirement. When unpopular decisions must be made, the good leader must be up-front about the facts, mindful of negative repercussions, and prepared to deal with the outcomes. The temptation to sugar-coat a message to prevent conflict does not make a problem go away; it only makes it worse.

Loyalty is something that we generally think of as going up the organisational tree, but it's not a one-way street. In order for loyalty to permeate an organisation, it must go both ways. The secret is that loyalty is most effective when it is shown to subordinates first. When a group knows the leadership has their best interests at heart, they show gratitude and loyalty. A leader shows loyalty in the way he or she represents the organisation. Leaders are mindful of the workload they impose on their group, and must be aware of inequities in the rate of effort. A good leader also ensures the group understands why a particular course of action has been taken. In this way, loyalty is shown both up and down the chain of command. Individuals are more likely to show loyalty and a strong work ethic if they believe their interests are being taken care of.

Initiative is linked to motivation, and leaders exhibit it in a variety of ways. A good leader recognises an opportunity when it presents, whether it has come by fortune or by design. Initiative is also linked to time, as the correct decision made at the correct time can pay disproportionate dividends. At a basic level, a good leader evaluates the situation that presents itself before acting. Upon assuming command of a new group or organisation, leaders should seek to understand the capabilities of people in their care. They actively get to know their people, learn their strengths and capabilities, and take note of their weaknesses or areas to improve. With this in mind, they can best employ their force as time goes on. Leaders also take the initiative to develop their team to become better. They involve other members of the leadership team to make this happen, which in turn develops their capabilities and performance. This is a form of continuous improvement, but improvements must be meaningful, and not done for appearance's sake. Of course, a leader also needs to show initiative in a contested environment. Leaders should recognise and seek to exploit weaknesses in their adversary—perhaps by filling a gap in a market, recruiting talent or initiating an ambush on an unsuspecting enemy. Taking the initiative in this way gives a leader the upper hand, and creates a platform for future success.

Judgement can be exercised in a variety of ways, and it's something we do every day without even thinking about it. We judge how long we have to drive to work, when to cross a road or how hard to run in a 5-kilometre race. As a leader, you are forced to make judgements every day to enable good decision-making. At a basic level, this might be related to the performance of your subordinates— regarding behaviour, fitness and accountability for their tasks. Judgement is required when choosing the best person to do a job, or who to promote to the next level of leadership. A leader must also exercise good tactical and strategic judgement. In the military, this means recognising the correct time to take—or not take—a decisive action, such as when to make a non-kinetic visit to a village where a battle has occurred, when to conduct the crossing of an obstacle that may be under observation or fire by the enemy, or when to clear a village or attack an enemy strongpoint. In a business setting, leaders must judge how and where to invest effort and finances—for example, whether adopting a new technology will create opportunities that did not exist previously. Good judgement is critical to good decision-making.

Ability to communicate is something that every leader must master. Leaders have to communicate their ideas to a variety of audiences. First and foremost, they deliver direction, orders and guidance to the people who work for them; they seek their opinions and use their knowledge and expertise to come up with a sensible plan. Leaders collaborate with their peers to ensure they are working well in concert and not inhibiting each other's efforts. Lastly, they must engage their commanders on the direction, orders and guidance they receive, and—when necessary—respectfully challenge their expectations and propose alternatives. This might be done verbally or in written form, but it is the manner in which it's delivered that makes a communication effective. Leaders need to get their ideas across in a way that brings everyone with them; they must be mindful of making adversaries when they're working to get people to understand, support or execute their plan. In my experience, the best way to communicate is verbally, face to face. A skilled communicator will be able to read the room by gauging people's reactions, asking for their input and getting instant feedback.

Knowledge is the aspect of leadership that underpins everything else. A leader needs to be in command of the relevant subject matter, but of course no single person can know everything. What's vital is to be aware of what you don't know and who you can ask to fill in your knowledge gap, and this requires humility and maturity. This is one of the most difficult things for a commander to do, especially if he or she has been a soldier and worked as a specialist. But leaders and commanders manage a collective capability. Their specialty, once they progress through the chain of command, is to know how best to employ the individuals and their individual capabilities in a collective environment. The collective knowledge they are charged with managing for the group is their most powerful weapon. Another key piece of knowledge for a leader is the tactics and strategy they need to be successful. They must understand the battlespace operating systems of friend and foe alike, and seek to advantage their own at the same time as neutralising the opposition's.

———

These eleven principles of leadership together form a set of standards and guidelines to help you make good decisions. You must decide which ones you apply, and at what time. Sometimes you'll need to call on all of them; at other times perhaps only one or two. Each command and leadership problem requires a unique solution. Use the time you have available and the principles outlined here to make the right decision.

LESSONS

Remember these principles using the acronym CMDR SILI JAK.

Courage in the face of danger is valuable, but so is the courage to stand up for your people and your principles.

Motivation gets you up and going, and inspires the people around you to do the same.

Decisiveness is the core tenet of leadership, as ultimately decisions must be made by the person in charge.

Responsibility flows from the decisions you make, whether good or bad; you are accountable to your superiors, peers and subordinates.

Selflessness is practised almost continually by a leader, in their dedication to tasks and in making their people their top priority.

Integrity in a leader builds trust, and without it a leader will fail to influence their group.

Loyalty must be shown to the people we lead; if we do so, they will repay it tenfold.

Initiative must be taken by the leader in everything they do, whether to secure a tactical advantage, to develop a subordinate, or to reward the group after a long week of work.

Judgement is required of a leader every day, as their decisions affect not only them but also the people they lead.

Ability to communicate enables a leader both to instruct subordinates effectively and to make best use of their feedback.

Knowledge is critical to a leader's success, and subordinates will judge them accordingly. If you don't know the answer, you should consult someone who does.

20

TYPES OF LEADERS

'To each there comes in their lifetime a special moment when they
are figuratively tapped on the shoulder and offered the chance
to do a very special thing, unique to them and fitted to their
talents. What a tragedy if that moment finds them unprepared or
unqualified for that which could have been their finest hour.'

Winston Churchill

In my opinion, the two best personal traits for leaders to have are
optimism and a tireless work ethic. Optimism is a great leadership
tool, and goes a long way towards motivating your subordinates,
helping you gain influence. It takes a lot of energy, though. The
commander with a relentless work ethic also injects his or her energy
into their leadership. As long as this work ethic is for the greater
good, it's also a very effective way to influence a team.

I'd like to introduce you to two leaders I've worked for. I think of
them as Lieutenant Optimism and Major Work Ethic.

————

My platoon commander in Somalia in 1993 was Lieutenant Vince
Creagh. Vince was just a few years older than me, but mentally he
was a long way ahead.

Vince was the commander of 4 Platoon, Bravo Company.
Our battalion was deploying on operations for the first time since

Vietnam, and Vince was excited. We were a young platoon, with an average age of just 24 or so. I was just nineteen.

Vince was easy-going and everyone liked him. He played rugby, liked a drink and was a man's man. I looked up to him. His leadership style was participative—Vince mucked in with his team as much as he could. When we began preparing for operations, though, and then during the tour, I noticed a change in him. He became much more positive and energetic. It's not that he wasn't before, but the shift was noticeable. I think Vince volunteered us for everything, or so it felt. He was collaborative, too, which I hadn't experienced before then.

He spent a lot of time with each of us personally and cared about our welfare. In many ways, our whole experience as a platoon in Somalia that year was shaped by Vince. Had we had a platoon commander who was less optimistic and attentive, we would not have fared so well mentally. I'm not saying we all got through unscathed, but it could have been worse.

In the early hours of Anzac Day 1993, at around 2 am, we were patrolling a dark street in the city of Baidoa. I was our platoon's forward scout. As I moved down the street, hugging the wall on the right-hand side for protection, a man walked out of a doorway ahead of me. He was smoking a cigarette and laughing with someone behind him, in the hallway. He noticed me too, and turned quickly to his right as he came down the steps. He seemed startled for a moment, then he tried to walk away at speed.

I yelled out to him in Somali to stop, and he did. He stood there frozen.

I approached him from behind, when suddenly he spun around and hit me in the stomach. I thought he hit me twice, but when I looked down I realised the first hit was a submachine gun being thrust into my guts. The second hit was from the bolt going forward, but the weapon did not fire the round: the firing pin had not hit the primer in the round hard enough for it to ignite the powder and fire the projectile.

I grabbed his left shoulder and brought up my weapon to engage him, but my rifle muzzle wedged under his armpit, with the barrel pointing down the street.

He was strong—stronger than me—and we struggled. He was trying to cock his weapon in order to clear the stoppage, while I was fighting to get my muzzle into his guts so I could let rip with a magazine. I was in a fight for my life—my first. The problem was that I was losing it.

I was in trouble, so I did what came naturally to me back then: I took the fight to the ground. Down there I could lock him up, choke his throat perhaps, grip him from the side and wrap his limbs up and negate his weapon. I swept his legs out and we crashed to the ground. I trapped his weapon under me and had my arm across his throat. I lay all my weight across his head and chest.

Then BOOM! The biggest, baddest guy in the battalion, who happened to be in my platoon back then, kicked this guy with so much force that it lifted us both. Then he kicked him again for good measure. His boots were size 13. He had seen the situation unfold and came in at speed to assist; I'd never been happier to see him.

We took the Somali guy's weapon. He was in no shape to resist at that point, so he was detained and left moaning on the steps under guard. I went back to the front of the section and took up a security position while the section cleared the house he'd come out of.

A few minutes later there was a commotion down another side street, an area that our number one rifleman was covering. There was some shouting, and then a weapon was fired, once, possibly twice. I ran to the shooting and found the rifleman kneeling there, covering a Somali man and a girl. I rushed over to assist and saw a weapon by the Somali, so I approached carefully and moved the weapon away.

My memory of that night isn't great, and I don't want to go into too many details. Suffice it to say the incident was confronting. I couldn't assist the injured Somali, as I was overwhelmed by the sight and sounds and started throwing up. The guy who'd come to my assistance on the other street rendered first aid to the Somali.

I didn't realise it at the time, but the confronting scene would become a frame of reference for me in the future. I was being battle-inoculated. Somalia either inoculated you or broke you, I understood in the years that followed.

When we arrived back at base that Anzac Day morning, Vince spoke to each of us. He was concerned about us, but he was positive in the way he approached our experiences and how we had acquitted ourselves. I was given some counselling by the Padre, by the second-in-command and by Vince, as were the others who'd been involved. Then we had a rum and a coffee for Anzac Day, and got on with the business we were there to do.

We didn't really speak of these incidents again as a platoon, which was a shame as it was a profound experience. Vince's leadership brimmed with optimism and energy. He didn't hide the fact that the expectations of us were high, but he also showed us that we could survive Somalia—that we were up to the task. He was a great platoon commander. His secret weapon was his optimism.

————

In 2008, the Officer in Command of Alpha Company, 4RAR Commando, was Major F. I'll refer to him in this story as Major Work Ethic.

I was a captain and the operations officer under Major Work Ethic. We prepared for service in Afghanistan for six months, and I can't remember a day that I beat him into work. He was always there before 7 am, working at his desk. He always left after me, too—I'm not even sure what time.

He had three platoons to worry about, and all the attachments, and he'd watch their training daily. He was across everyone's job, mine included, and I tried to match his work ethic. During the mission rehearsal exercise, he set up tasks that were realistic, and the time spans replicated what we would face. It seemed he hardly ever slept, and he certainly helped everyone get better in their roles.

A bit like Lieutenant Creagh, Major Work Ethic changed in the lead-up to our deployment. His hours extended, his application to his work increased, and he took it very seriously. He set the tone for the company, so we all took it very seriously too. The platoon commanders worked tirelessly, as did I and the second-in-command.

The stakes were high. In 2008, people weren't coming home, and many of the personnel killed in Afghanistan were commandos. We were the tip of the spear—or the sledgehammer, as we liked to refer to ourselves.

I remember one mission particularly well. It was to be a night raid on a compound of interest many miles away. We started planning days ahead, and worked long hours into the night. There was map reconnaissance to be done, and we had to present the back brief on the proposed mission. The course of action took the best part of a day to prepare, and it was presented to the Commanding Officer for approval. The orders were written and refined and then presented. We conducted rehearsal-of-concept drills out on the ground, and actions were practised and refined. By the time the company was ready to deploy, I was exhausted.

The enemy always gets a vote on your plans—that's one of the rules of war—but the enemy's vote didn't amount to much in this instance, given the preparation that had gone into our operation. The company inserted by helicopter, miles from the target, and walked most of the night to reach the compound of interest. The commandos returned home with the prisoners they went there for, and those who had violently resisted were killed and left behind. The operation was a success, and would serve as a template for direct-action strikes in the future.

A key factor in the plan being so bulletproof was Major Work Ethic's firm grip on the reins of the company, and his clear articulation of what we were there to do. The company was very successful on Special Operations Task Group Rotation 7 due in part to the energy he brought to his work. He was a master in all leadership skill domains—interpersonal skills, conceptual skills, technical skills and operational skills—and his work ethic was unmatched. This was his leadership secret weapon.

———

Leaders apply the principles of leadership in different ways to come up with unique solutions. At the various rank and command levels, leaders must lead in different ways. Sometimes it's a hands-on approach, sometimes leading by example, and sometimes a more authoritarian style is required. The operating environment dictates the best solution. Good leaders understand this, and moderate the way they interact with their organisation accordingly.

LESSONS

The two best personal traits for leaders to have are optimism and a tireless work ethic.

In Somalia, Lieutenant Creagh was able to influence his men by transferring his optimistic approach to them. We did what he wanted because we wanted to do it for him.

Major Work Ethic, along with mastery of all leadership skills, had an unmatched work ethic. This was his secret weapon for generating influence among his men.

21

LEADERSHIP IN ACTION

'We are what we pretend to be, so we must be
careful about what we pretend to be.'

Kurt Vonnegut

Great leaders understand that it's all about energy transference—
from them to their people. They need to span the spectrum from
empathy to exuberance. Some people will follow you easily, some will
require evidence that what you're asking is the right way to go, some
will need to be bashed into submission (figuratively speaking), and,
finally, some will need you to make the decision to cut them away
and let them drift off because they were never worth your time.

I've been lucky to have had some great leaders, and I have seen
the worst of them too. What I find interesting about the topic of
leadership is how most theorists discuss its intricacies as if it were
occurring in a vacuum. They talk about changing your leadership
style to suit the person or the situation, but this only really works in a
one-on-one interaction, when the person is open to being led. People
in the real world don't often behave like this.

I've come around to the idea that leadership is about 'place'.
I could actually write a whole book just on this subject. What I mean
by 'place' isn't just the physical place that you're in, although the
environment certainly does play a part. The 'place' I'm referring to
is where you are along your journey as a leader and as a person, and
where the recipient is on their journey. The physical place might be

out on the firing range. It could be morning or it could be afternoon; either of these could affect the outcome of the interaction. You could be tired, or perhaps you're well rested. You might be feeling resilient or your resilience might be low due to a lack of sleep or exposure to the elements. You may be thirsty, or perhaps you're hungry. The other person could be affected by all these variables as well. So, what works in one interaction will almost certainly not net the same results in another similar interaction because of the subtle differences of 'place'. Leadership therefore becomes more about 'place' than about style and you have to change your approach depending on the 'place'.

Much harder than dealing with just one person is developing the skills to inspire small teams made up of introverts, extroverts and everyone in between. Being an effective leader would be simpler if we were handed a Myers–Briggs Type Indicator assessment for everyone in our team.

In an infantry platoon you'll find a diverse range of personalities, experiences and backgrounds—and that's just what's on the surface. Sexuality, gender identification, multicultural alignment, religious practices—all these require consideration.

Small group dynamics and leadership go hand-in-hand. Every time you stand up in front of a group, you might be followed or commit leadership suicide. Trust is hard to earn and easy to lose. Competence in a subject is hard to project and easily questioned. It's highly likely someone in your team is smarter than you, or an expert in the area that you're in charge of. Honesty and integrity are personality traits that require constant reassessment, because your words and actions offer constant evidence. Say the wrong thing to the wrong person—or, worse still, let someone get away with something that impacts the whole team—and the next time you stand in front of your team, their faces will tell the story of your betrayal.

It's said that leadership is a lonely business. I agree—it is. I've met non-commissioned officers and commissioned officers who subscribe to the notion that leadership is all about mateship. They assume that to get the most out of your team, you have to be their friend. Moreover, the weak leader thinks that the benevolent leader is one who has the trust of his mates—that they'll do anything for you if they like you. This isn't the Army's leadership model, I might add. And sometimes, regardless of the world-class training you've received, and even when pointed in the right direction by numerous mentors, one still has to learn things the hard way.

———

When I was a young commando corporal in charge of a section, I had an encounter that changed my life in many ways. My second-in-charge, or 2IC, was a man who was to become my best friend during my career, and is still one of my closest friends. He was a very astute and well-rounded commando, with high proficiency in all the areas in which I was weaker, so we complemented each other well.

When he arrived at the unit, no one wanted him as their 2IC because he was a reserve commando. But as a reservist, he had definitely put in the work. He had more experience in certain areas than any of the newly qualified regulars, yet still some couldn't see past their prejudices. I had a ten-minute conversation with him and realised that he was what I needed. I met with my company commander, and the next thing I knew I had 'inherited their rubbish' and was in charge of training him. Even the officers couldn't see the great asset we had received.

In 1998, we were involved in a competition organised by the battalion. All the sections were to conduct the same full mission profile to determine which was the best section in the newly formed 4RAR Commando. It would be hotly contested.

The event ran something like this. The section commander received orders from the company commander, while the section 2IC conducted the battle preparation with the soldiers, including some first-aid tests and skill-at-arms tests. Then the section commander would give his orders. We were to move from Holsworthy Barracks down to the Georges River, where we would assemble two F470 Zodiac boats—an inflatable used by Special Forces worldwide for its seaworthiness, low signature and compact size.

We would conduct a night transit along the river, out to Botany Bay, out of the heads and north up the coast, past Palm Beach and onto one of the small islands at the mouth of the Hawkesbury River. There we would cache our boats and move inland to recover a downed pilot, before returning to the boats and transiting back to Holsworthy Barracks. All of this was to be completed in 24 hours, and without detection by an enemy force who could be anywhere along the route.

My section had its share of good to very good commandos, and while we were probably underdogs, I knew we were capable of victory. I was friends with the guys in the section and I knew their strengths and weaknesses. We were particularly good at nautical navigation, as my 2IC was an amphibious operations supervisor and instructor and so highly competent at this skill. I let him run this aspect of the mission without interference or question.

I developed our tactical plan and the actions to be carried out once we were delivered to the island. I focused on the crux of the problem: locating and recovering the downed pilot, and evading enemy contact.

We decided not to bury our boats above the waterline or hide them in the undergrowth, both of which would take time and effort. I say we, because I was using a collaborative leadership style: I presented the problems and we went around the group for solutions. We weighed up the risk versus the reward of maintaining a floating cache, outside of visual distance, and leaving two guys with the boats. If we were going to win the competition, we had to be creative and bold.

This would become a characteristic of my leadership through-out the years. I always aspired to be a leader like those of the Special Forces during World War Two. There's no point applying conventional solutions when you're part of a non-conventional force. War isn't a game, but it still needs to be played. While this attitude was one of my strengths, it would also create friction with some senior commanders in years to come.

The night transit along the Georges River went well, and before dawn we'd arrived at the target location. We disembarked and crept slowly through the bushland. We followed a track to the grid refer-ence and located the hiding pilot, who had been conducting his escape and evasion plan. He was in the undergrowth just outside an old building. We went through the marry-up plan and validated the codes required for him to show himself. The whole time we had a judge following us around, marking me on my performance and my team on theirs.

We began moving back to the boats, with Alpha Team (my team) in the lead and Bravo Team (my 2IC's team) following. The men were in staggered file along the track; my two scouts were leading, then me. As we went, I noticed that my forward scout was carrying his rifle by the handle as he sauntered down the bush track to the beach. I let it slide. The number two scout was patrolling properly, as was everyone else, so even though it pissed me off, it wasn't that big of a deal—or so I thought.

But the judge had seen it too. In fact, as I found out later, my whole team had seen it, and in time the whole section would come to know about it. The judge took a dim view of the scout not playing the game, and an even dimmer view of me not fixing the issue.

The young soldier was a country boy, and naturally talented in the bush. That's why he was a scout—and he was good at his job. He was a simple guy, too, not academically smart but definitely not stupid. He didn't like authority, especially the authority of a commander of his own age. I'd had trouble with him for months, almost needing to beg him to do things that I asked.

In my leadership experience, he's the most memorable failure— and probably my best learning experience, too. I wanted him to like me, to respect me and to do what he was fucking told. But when it mattered, during the section competition, I didn't have the courage to call him out. I failed myself and, as it turned out, I failed the whole section. The ramifications of this would be immense.

We finished the competition, and all in all I felt we'd done a great job. My 2IC was praised for his advanced navigation and nautical skills, and I was praised for my planning, orders and tactics. We had finished hours ahead of any of the other sections and had been bold in our execution.

The section commanders were assembled a few days later to receive the results. Our Commanding Officer and regimental sergeant major stood in front of us to announce the placings. The teams that came third and fourth were two of my biggest threats, led by inspiring commanders who, in years to come, would become institutions within the commando community. Then I and one other guy were asked to come to the front. We were first and second, but the order was unclear.

The other guy won. He would go on to become a leader within the Special Air Service Regiment (SASR). We'd come from the 1st Battalion of the Royal Australian Regiment together, and he became a lifelong friend. His section had come first by a few points. We shook hands and that was that. He was given the choice of a commendation or a trip to the United Kingdom to serve as an instructor at the Royal Marines Training Centre. He chose the commendation as he was preparing to join the SASR. That left me to head off to the UK.

I returned to my section to tell them we had come second—and I shared the exciting news that I'd received an all-expenses-paid trip overseas for a year. I told them how proud I was of their performance, and how they'd done a great job but we'd been beaten by a better team.

They stared back at me, disappointment written on their faces. A question came: 'How much did we fucking lose by, Conno?'

It hadn't been asked in a very respectful way, but I let that go through to the keeper.

'Not much at all,' I said happily. 'It was super close.'

They all looked back at me with hatred—no, it was worse than that: betrayal.

I couldn't compute what I was seeing. We'd all worked so hard—except that one guy, perhaps—and we'd only just lost. And I won a trip! Then it dawned on me: we had lost because I hadn't stepped up when it counted. They had needed a true leader, not a section commander, and I had failed. They would only have won bragging rights, but that meant everything to them—and now I was being rewarded. It was praise for my weakness.

Leadership truly is a lonely business sometimes, especially if you get it wrong.

Some people you have to lead are exhausting and will erode your effectiveness if you don't manage their personality. How do you lead someone like that? It took me years to work it out. When it's your job to lead a group of people with different agendas and personalities, you must lead with empathy for some and exuberance for others. When you encounter someone who simply doesn't want to be led, or who wants to fight you because you're the leader—well, you must compel them to submit. Leadership can be combative at times, and some people simply have to be bludgeoned until they toe the line.

I was asked recently by someone still serving in the Army if I could provide a few strategies on how not to be jaded by leadership. I reminded that person that they were in fact the Army and that they should take the opportunities to show how professionals lead. It's too easy to blame an organisation for the shortfalls of a few and to fall into the trap of becoming a leader who makes everyone else feel jaded as well.

I've also encountered the guy who just needs to be cut adrift. You need to be aware that these people exist, and be prepared to come down hard when it's required. This is where moral courage is essential. The effect of letting people get away with undermining you will mean the whole team suffers in the long run.

———

Can a leader be friends with their subordinates? I get asked this question a lot. As I said before, some people firmly believe that friendships undermine the effectiveness of the leader. I think that position is too simplistic and doesn't allow for the complexities of human behaviour and the importance of the leader/subordinate relationship.

A friend is someone you know well and share a mutual affection with. Given this definition, it's easy to see why some believe friendships undermine a leader's authority. A relationship based on mutual affection can cause a leader to show favouritism to the friend over others on the team. But *not* being friends with your subordinates can be even more problematic.

If leadership means getting someone to want to do what you need them to do, then it stands to reason that it's easier to accomplish this if you can compel those with whom you share a mutual affection. Being a leader to your friends can be very effective indeed. Of course, it comes with complexities, but that doesn't mean you should sever all personal ties with your subordinates.

As a leader, you can choose between a directive, participative and delegative leadership style, and moderate your style depending on the situation or the interaction. The same goes for your interactions with your subordinates. At times you need to demonstrate empathy, and at other times you should be firm. Without doubt there will be times when you have to make tough decisions that are blind to your friendships. It's all about the professionalism of both leader and subordinate.

LESSONS

You can't apply the same style of leadership to everyone in your organisation, as individuals are motivated and inspired by different things and respond to direction in different ways.

'Place' is all about where you are as a leader and all the variables that are affecting you (and those you're leading) at any given time. 'Place' is the most difficult concept to understand, but once you do, your leadership ability is increased exponentially.

Try to bring everybody on the journey. Make them feel valued and part of the team success, and not ostracised. Don't cause them to feel they should challenge you without good reason.

Success for the leader does not mean success for the group. If the team is successful then the leader has been successful, but the reverse is not necessarily true.

22

LEADING LEADERS

'The greatest leader is not necessarily the one who
does the greatest things. He is the one that gets
the people to do the greatest things.'

Ronald Reagan

Identifying the micro influencers within a team is critical to a well-rounded leadership strategy. If you don't lead leaders, they will undermine you. If you lead them well, they will support you before you even ask. Another important aspect of good leadership is setting the right example for future leaders. There's nothing like learning from experience, as I discovered throughout my career.

———

Timor Leste, 9 September 2001. I adjusted my night-vision googles to gain a clearer picture of the animal walking along the track. I couldn't believe my eyes. My forward scout had seen it as well, and he slowly raised his hand to adjust the focal lens of his goggles.

Just before nightfall, I'd manoeuvred my six-man reconnaissance team into a position at the edge of some lantana and adjacent to a small track that animals used to move to and from a watercourse. It was clear to me now that this track was also a primary hunting area for the animal I was now observing.

The night before, we had been a twelve-man commando section. I was in command and had set up in an ambush position on a walking track that led away from the tactical control line (TCL), which in this case was the riverbed separating East and West Timor. My men were tired after a week spent patrolling the border, looking for incursions by returning rebels or members of the Indonesian Special Forces, Kopassus.

My second-in-charge was an ex-SASR trooper who had left that unit under a cloud. Unfortunately, he was now a fully quali-fied corporal in my commando section, and was turning out to be a right pain in the arse. He had been testing my resolve for weeks, and making my experience of leadership a lot harder than it needed to be. At times, it felt like I was in a race to win the guys over. There was no collaboration, just competition, and it was wearing thin on me.

We had moved silently through the low scrub and secondary jungle approaches to the border, and then conducted a fishhook drill, patrolling back over the way we had just walked to ensure we hadn't been followed up. These drills were intuitive to me, as I'd spent so much time in the jungle when in 1RAR. But the effort that I was making to avoid the enemy was freaking my 2IC out.

When I look back on this experience now, I wonder if I scared him by being so concerned about Kopassus fighters. I was almost obsessed with finding them, and with not being found by them. This urge drove my every decision.

I went forward to conduct the reconnaissance with my two scouts, leaving the 2IC in charge of the rest of the section. I had briefed him thoroughly on the 'actions on' that we would conduct, should either location come into contact with the enemy. His eyes were like dinner plates as I went through the different permutations of the plan, if contact occurred.

I retuned about twenty minutes later and found the 2IC deep in conversation with one of the other members of the section. I'd been having issues with this team member too since becoming a section commander. It was the guy who had cost us the section competition two years prior, and his abruptness and at times disregard for my authority had made him almost unmanageable.

If the two of them got a foothold in the section and gained some leverage over me, it would erode my effectiveness. Worse still, I could find myself hit with a vote of no confidence by the men—a death blow to any junior commander. I was already uncomfortable about the power the 2IC was wielding due to his SASR experience, and I didn't know how to deal with him. After a little thought, I decided I would bludgeon the two of them into submission.

I had always been a natural-born leader, but at this early stage of my career I didn't understand leadership. In fact, many of the officers who had led me had probably experienced what I was now suffering with these two muppets. As a younger soldier, I would call out decisions publicly, or profess to know better, or even undermine my leaders behind their backs. Between 1994 and 1999, no one had deployed anywhere, but I'd been in a privileged crew that had been to Somalia. I touted this experience like it made me some magical warfighter.

I was embarrassed about my behaviour at this time. But I needed these experiences to become a better leader in the future. A good leader must also know what it is to be led. It got to the point that I learnt plenty about leadership theory from the subtle things I was doing to undermine my superiors.

I gave my final orders to the section and we prepared to move out and occupy the ambush location. In my mind, our mission was easy. I wanted the guys to be ready to kill or capture any enemy element that patrolled through our ambush location.

I had done this operationally numerous times before, in Somalia. I was a forward scout back then, and my section commander had been aggressive. We would set up ambushes everywhere, with the sole intent of killing anyone stupid enough to creep around with a weapon. I had completed many an ambush lesson in the infantry battalions too; I'd spent more time conducting ambushes than attacks, in fact. I was good at this; it was my thing.

The 2IC didn't like my orders. I was being too aggressive, he argued. 'I'm uncomfortable with this,' he said. 'I don't think we should be doing it.' I ignored him at first, but when he persisted I started to get pissed off. Finally, I took him out of the gun group in the ambush and put him in the rear protection group, as much to get him away from me as to placate him.

We lay there all night and waited. Earlier in the evening, some baboons made their way along the track. They stopped short of us and sniffed the air. Their approaching footsteps had sounded very much like an enemy force conducting a tactical movement. It had been unsettling at first until they came close enough that we could distinguish them. We watched them move past us, sixteen sets of eyes fixed on them until they disappeared.

The rest of the night was uneventful. Just another warm night on an island north of Australia, and nothing significant to report. It was my Timor experience in a nutshell. When dawn threatened, I made the call to collapse the ambush location and fold back to the patrol base, where we'd have breakfast and work out our patrol plan for the day ahead.

Once we'd finished the morning routine, I gave orders to my section. We would be splitting up: my 2IC's team was to head inland, towards the next night's extraction location, while I would take my team and set up some listening posts in and around the TCL.

I had wanted to separate the section for some time, but had only just been authorised by the platoon commander to conduct two team tasks instead of one larger one. The 2IC seemed happy about it too. But deep down I felt I had failed at something, even if I wasn't sure what it was.

The following night, I sat in my tactical lay-up position thinking about the last few weeks. We had almost finished conducting quiet time, where we would tune in to our surroundings before slowly, one at a time, pulling out a sleeping bag to gain a few hours' sleep. I had used the quiet time to think about the issue with my 2IC. What was his problem, I wondered.

Suddenly an uneasy feeling crept over me. Could I legally have ambushed anyone the previous day, given our rules of engagement? I wasn't sure. I suspected my 2IC knew the answer, and that he was uncomfortable about my obsession with the Indonesians and warfare in general. The more tactically I acted, the greater our chances of initiating a contact with the enemy. I thought more deeply about the strategic effect that a lethal ambush might have on our operations, and the second-order effect on international relations. Could it cause more harm than good? I started to feel embarrassed.

As I contemplated all this, I saw something stalking towards me—a feral cat, I thought. I watched the outline of this creature as it stealthily moved up the track. She moved with such stealth and grace—she was only a few metres away, but her every movement was completely silent. One foot would be raised and then placed gently down, no other body part moving. She was black, her tail was almost half as long as her entire body—and she was big. This was no feral cat, I suddenly understood; this was a leopard or jaguar or a similar creature.

She stopped and raised her head, drawing in one long smell, and then exploded away into the scrub. Two bounds at lightning speed and then there was silence. I wasn't the only one to see it, but I was the only one looking for a sign. I realised I had been so fixated on finding the enemy that I'd stopped paying attention to my surroundings, and in particular to the human dynamics in my section and team.

We extracted later the next day. Our platoon commander separated the sections into teams, and from then on we would rarely work with each other, the other teams, or myself and that section commander. My old section 2IC now had his own leadership challenges to deal with, and in some ways, I felt that I had failed him, by not demonstrating more of an example for him to follow. He would find his own way in years to come.

The next day was 11 September 2001. It changed our lives forever, and set me on a new path. The platoon was disbanded after Timor, and I departed to attend the first of the courses for the soon-to-be-raised TAG East.

————

Nine years after my Timor deployment, I found myself in Afghanistan, where my leadership would be critical to the outcome of many events. Plenty of water had gone under the bridge since Timor, and I'd learnt a different leadership style.

In 2009 I had returned to the National Counter Terrorist Team as the Sniper Platoon commander. My platoon was made up of the who's who of the sniper world within the 2nd Commando Regiment. I'd worked with many of these lads before. A few were from the Navy's Clearance Diving Branch, which exposed me to more people from different backgrounds and cultures.

I was told in October that I would be taking over as platoon commander of the Land Platoon (Yankee Platoon), and that we'd be deploying to Afghanistan early in 2010. They were just down the hall from my Sniper Platoon office, and a few of my men would also be joining the new platoon as its sniper detachment.

I had learnt over the last few years that leadership takes trust, and that building trust takes time. So I made it my business to get to know the guys even before I took over. During the handover with the outgoing platoon commander—a friend of mine and a man I had watched grow as a leader—I asked lots of questions, mostly about the commandos and their personalities.

Once I took over the platoon, I focused on showing my men that I could do the job. I demonstrated my competence by planning activities and organising my tactical acumen so that it could never be brought into question. By the time we deployed, we had conducted multiple missions and participated in the mission rehearsal exercise, where we were assessed. I felt I had built a high-performing team. I was building on the excellent work the previous platoon commander had done, and the commandos were working for me better than I'd dared to hope.

On day three or four in Afghanistan, we conducted a platoon vehicle patrol as we made our way south-east from Tarin Kowt towards Kandahar. I planned to get there in a couple of weeks. This was a disrupt mission, a patrol to keep the enemy on their toes, and to uncover intelligence. The guys didn't like these types of patrols, but I loved them. Being 'outside the wire' and in command was the stuff I'd dreamt of as a kid. This was a true desert patrol.

It was late afternoon when I called the platoon to stop. We had spent the day slowly moving forward, with the brave engineers from the Special Operations Engineer Regiment clearing a path for us through the desert valley. We'd discovered some Improvised Explosive Devices (IEDs) and had learnt that we were being monitored from a village up ahead.

For the last day we had also been shadowed by a Kuchi family. The Kuchi are a nomadic tribe native to Afghanistan, similar to the Bedouin of North Africa, the Arabian Peninsula, Iraq and the Levant. Like Bedouin, Kuchi use camels as beasts of burden, and travel with goats and sheep in tow as a food source and to trade. They had kept a safe distance behind us, and we knew the Taliban had been in contact with them to learn about our movements.

I loved this stuff—it was like chess with an enemy commander.

I dispatched two snipers to make contact with the Kuchi and take them some tea and biscuits. Our men wore some old goatherds' blankets over their uniforms, and rode a couple of beat-up Helmand 175 bikes that we had liberated from their bad guy owners. The snipers spent the day with the Kuchi, while another pair sat in overwatch, ready to blast any Taliban should they appear. I was still learning the art of subterfuge in warfare. Show the enemy one thing but do another; it had been done by Special Forces since their inception.

The snipers returned at the end of the afternoon, and the Kuchi happily strolled past the camp we had set up. I had located it a kilo-metre or so from a village, but behind a feature so they couldn't observe us all night. We were also far enough from the edge of the mountains that the enemy wouldn't be able to fire on us.

The night slowly engulfed my platoon. My platoon sergeant, Paul Cale, and I retreated to the back of the command vehicle and planned the next day's drive. We loaded the GPS maps, and we war-gamed scenarios while I wrote my orders. In the darkness, our men were conducting their nightly routine.

I enjoyed these evenings—these were the best days of my life, and I knew it at the time. That night I lay there on my back, looking up at the kaleidoscope of stars and pondering existence. Morning came—and I remember what happened next like it was yesterday. (Trigger warning—graphic content and explanations follow.)

I was standing there talking to Paul Cale and a few others. I had a coffee in my hand, and as we talked I watched one of the teams going about their business quietly packing their vehicle. Suddenly, from behind me, I heard a huge explosion. I quickly looked around the platoon but I had already assessed what it was. Some fucking stupid Taliban had just blown himself up setting an IED in the ground for us.

I could see the lads thinking the same thing. I was already formulating a response plan. I began shouting orders and rallying the troops, but seconds later there was another blast. Now I was search-ing my frames of reference for what that could possibly be, but my data base in this instance was empty. What the fuck was going on?

'Let's go!' I yelled. I gave a quick set of confirmatory orders: the first commando team would lead out at top speed, my team would follow close behind; there would be no clearance, no overwatch. Paul would follow with the engineers and clear a route to the point of the explosions. I had decided to sacrifice security for speed, but I wasn't going to let the whole platoon be drawn into what might be an ambush.

We responded within minutes, and as our lead vehicle rounded the corner, the team commander notified me that there were 'multiple KIA'—killed in action. We stopped and I jumped out, followed closely by my men.

The scene was apocalyptic. I saw two giant holes, and blood, guts and bone fragments everywhere. The commando team adopted a stance for all-round protection and watched for the enemy. Only metres away from where I stood were Kuchi family members. The women sat in a circle, wailing at the top of their lungs, and the young children were in shock wandering around the carnage. The old man of the tribe paced back and forth through the debris, chanting, '*Ill humdilliah*'—which means 'It is God's will'. Those words will forever haunt me, because I knew it had nothing to do with his god. Witnessing this event shaped me—as a person and as a leader. It also shaped my views on religion.

I saw a hand lying on the ground, and picked it up; it was from an adult male. I walked over and gave it to the old man, he looked at me and cried, holding the hand against his heart. He started pacing again.

The men in my platoon stood in silence and watched. We all knew the IEDs had been put there for us the day before. These Kuchi people had no knowledge of this. One of the old man's adult sons had been packing their camels when the younger camel stepped on the first IED. It had been placed in some old wheel tracks. The blast blew both the older and younger camel and the son to smithereens.

The second son had run down from their camp in a panic and had stepped on the second, larger IED, killing him instantly. That one had been laid to the side of the tracks.

In a matter of moments, this tribe had lost its young leaders. All that remained were women, babies, children and an old man. Fuck the world.

My intelligence corporal started picking up the tiny pieces of the men. I followed his example, and then the other men joined in. We found every piece of those two young men that could be recovered. One of the guys found the elder son's head a long the way down the track. The old man took it and held it, and the women surrounded him, sobbing and screaming.

While this was going on, one of my teams went to the village and knocked on every door. Eventually we found bomb-making equipment, homemade explosives and everything needed to set up IEDs all over the valley. We were told that the Taliban had escaped on a motorbike to the south; we were told what they were wearing and where they would be heading.

I was so impressed by my men's actions that day. They did what I wanted them to do because they wanted to do it, and without me asking. The leaders in the group had learnt to lead their own men in the same way that I led them. We had a common purpose, and whenever there was an issue we acted and reacted as one. I had learnt to lead through influence.

The bomb-making building was levelled by an air strike later that day. For the next two days we collected intelligence as we moved down the valley with speed to cut off the Taliban's escape routes. We used every piece of sophisticated technology that a modern Army can bring to bear on an 'enemy. Finally, on the third day, two Taliban fighters who had left the area on a motor bike were targeted for a drone strike. I saw to their demise and felt nothing. It took me years to feel anything again.

We gave the Kuchi everything we could: all of our patrol cash, tarpaulins, clothes and food. But we also knew, as they headed off after the burial the next day, that they would need a miracle to survive. With no young men, and with the very real possibility that the Taliban would find out we had provided them with support, I'd be surprised if there is one person left alive from that family today.

LESSONS

A good leader will evolve and improve over time, both through conscious self-improvement and because of maturity and experience.

Mentoring junior leaders under your command is important for their development and yours—even if they are proving difficult. A problematic subordinate simply means additional effort is required of a leader.

When you have matured as a leader and put in the effort, you will be rewarded with a team that channels your vision and puts it into action without you needing to demand it.

23

KNOW YOUR PEOPLE

'I suppose leadership at one time meant muscles;
but today it means getting along with people.'

Mahatma Gandhi

As a leader, knowing your people on a personal level ensures you can connect with them in a meaningful way. A deeper connection builds trust, enhancing your ability to influence them to help you achieve your mission. And I mean you have to know more than just someone's work persona. You need to understand them as an individual: their personality, their quirks, their strengths and their weaknesses. Only then can you build a meaningful connection with them.

Back in 1997, when I was participating in the very first selection course for the Australian Army's modern commando capability, I received a very direct lesson in the value of getting to know your team.

'What's your platoon sergeant's name?' Major Hans Fleer boomed.

The sound of his voice was like a foghorn in the mist of the winter morning. A crackle of cockatoos took flight, squawking and flapping as his words echoed across the damp valley.

When I think back to Hans now, it's with great admiration—and, if I'm honest, a degree of love too. The way a son loves a father. You see, Hans Fleer was like no one else I'd ever met. His legend was known across special operations and I was in awe of him.

'He's killed more men than cholera' was a regular comment made of him. 'If Darth Vader and Chuck Norris had a lovechild, it'd be Hans Fleer' was another. He had nicknames such as 'The Dark Prince' or 'The Dark Lord', 'The Phantom' and even 'God', but most knew him as 'The Iceman'.

One year not long after my selection, I had a scary encounter with Hans. I was the guard commander and doing my rounds at about 2 am. There had been some break-ins around the unit in recent times: a lot of shiny equipment and the lack of any real boundary fence had created an opportunity for thieves. I saw a light in the Commando Training Wing headquarters. The front door was open and music was playing, but too gently for me to make out what it was.

I crept in, ghost-walking down the hallway. My commando beret sloped forward, and with my large torch at the ready I inched closer to the end of the corridor. I tilted my head around the doorframe so that just my eye was exposed.

The music playing was 'Send in the Clowns' by Stephen Sondheim, haunting at the best of times. Hans sat behind a computer screen, his face illuminated in the blueish light. A shadow extending across his face cast a sinister reflection against the wall behind him. Involuntarily, I shivered.

'Yes, Corporal Connolly?' Hans said quietly, without taking his eyes from the screen.

I stepped into the doorway and swallowed hard. 'Good morning, sir. I . . . I saw the door was open. I just wanted to check that the place was secure.'

Hans continued typing for what seemed like a lifetime, completing whatever thought it was that I had interrupted.

'I think we both know the security status of this building, don't we, Corporal Connolly?' he said finally. I thought I saw the glimmer of a smirk as he spoke.

I took a step back, turned and walked out of the building and down the path. Turning for a moment, I glanced back at the Training Wing HQ. It was now completely dark. The door was shut and nothing moved. The wind didn't even whisper past my ears. Everything was calm.

What on earth? How was that possible?

I glanced up at the climbing tower—a friend, my refuge, and the place I had mastered over the past year—and felt a sense of calm wash over me. Hans always had a way of helping you find clarity.

Back to selection in 1997, and Hans putting a young officer on the spot. Did he know his platoon sergeant's name?

'Sergeant, sir,' the platoon commander replied nervously. 'It's Sergeant or Sarge.'

This isn't going to end well, I thought. I was yet to see if Hans had any semblance of a sense of humour and now the young lieutenant was proving that was not to be the case. A few minutes earlier we'd been marching to the top of a hill around 15 kilometres out of Lithgow. We'd been walking since midnight, labouring under huge packs. It hadn't rained—we'd had all that in the first week of selection. For the first three days we'd been trapped in Bulahdelah, lying under our hoochies waiting for the rain to subside so we could begin the selection course proper.

'Hans organised that,' we had joked. 'To grind us down before we begin.'

Now Hans stooped to bring his mouth near the platoon commander's ear. 'What are your section commanders' names?' he asked softly.

'Corporal Connolly, Corporal Smith and Corporal Taylor,' the young officer replied.

'*What are any of your soldiers' names?*' Now he was yelling. '*What are their wives' names, their kids' names, their dogs' names? And I mean their first names!*'

It was the first and only time I'd ever heard the Dark Prince's voice raised. My heart stopped for a moment. Looking around at the platoon, I could see everyone else in a state of shock too.

Of course, when the Land Rover had come up the winding mud track, slipping and sliding its way towards us, we had become nervous. Perhaps it was bringing us egg and bacon rolls and hot coffee, I had suggested, and I'd tried to spread this positive thought across my section. But when Hans had stepped out, his cams perfectly pressed, his jungle boots reflectively polished and his Sherwood green beret perfectly adorning his head, we knew we were in the shit. His sudden presence could only mean a new task, a change of plan or most likely someone's demise.

Our platoon commander's eyes darted around as he searched for answers. He had suddenly grasped the urgency of the situation, was struggling to understand how he'd got into this position, and he didn't possess the tools to get himself out of it. He wiped the sweat from his brow; even in freezing temperatures, Hans could make you sweat.

Finally Hans Fleer extended his arm and placed his hand on the young infantry officer's shoulder. 'Lieutenant, please retrieve your equipment, then seat yourself in the back of this vehicle.' Hans never took his eyes off the man as he spoke.

The young officer walked back to the platoon position, his head hanging low. Picking up his pack, he shot me a sideways glance and then turned to walk away. He heaved his pack into the back of the green Land Rover and clambered inside. He sat with his elbows on his knees and his head in his hands. All the platoon members were now on their feet, and we had a sense of dread hanging over us.

Hans scanned the men's faces while rubbing his chin in thought, surveying the effect of his lesson on his audience. He turned and got into the driver's seat of the vehicle.

We watched as the car bounced its way down the hill. The engine noise died out some minutes later, and an eerie silence settled over the valley. I was emotionally wrecked. I felt like I'd witnessed some violent action, yet it had just been a conversation.

I locked eyes with one of my mates, Corporal Taylor. We had worked with each other for a bit over a year now. 'Tails, what's your fucking first name?' I blurted out.

'It's Max, mate. What's yours?'

This pattern was repeated across the platoon, as every guy started learning as much as possible about the others. Even when we finally started walking again, we kept talking. First names, wives' names, kids and pets. Nothing was off-limits.

Over the weeks of the selection course, we became a tight unit. We lost more guys along the way—many guys, actually. But those who remained became close and knew a lot about each other. The guys who were successful are friends of mind to this day. As for the young platoon commander—we never saw him again . . . ever.

Colonel Johannes Cornelis Fleer AM, DCM would become the Honorary Colonel for the 2nd Commando Regiment. I'm struggling to write these next sentences through the tears of loss. He died of melanoma on 5 April 2013, aged 63. Hans had survived two tours of Vietnam, separated by only a few weeks' leave. During one engagement with the Viet Cong, he ran out into the line of enemy fire to begin the recovery of nine critically wounded soldiers. Everyone who witnessed it believed it to be a suicide mission.

Hans' most notable qualities were humility, integrity and honesty. It's no coincidence that these are the essential qualities of a leader— not just a boss or a manager, but a true leader. Every interaction I ever had with Hans made me a better leader and, more importantly, a better person. He is sorely missed.

LESSONS

If you don't know your people, you'll miss the cues that reveal their wellbeing, and fail to appreciate what makes them tick. You won't get the best out of them until you correct this.

Taking an interest in your people's lives will be rewarding for you as a leader too. Forging a meaningful connection will influence your subordinates to support you and the missions and tasks you are given.

VALUES

24

HONESTY

'If you tell the truth, you don't have
to remember anything.'

Mark Twain

In our day-to-day interactions, we are given many opportunities to act tactically, think operationally and plan strategically. If you get these in the wrong order, there can be second-order effects that you didn't visualise. Get them in the right order and you can effect significant change.

By way of example, let me tell you about one occasion when I had to be disingenuous with my partner force to achieve a positive result and a strategic effect. I wasn't left with too many options by the partner force commander when he demanded I hand over a drug haul to him. It would have been simpler to take the easy wrong over the hard right, so I had to show a degree of cunning. Honesty is vital in leadership—it is the platform for integrity—so I advise you to be careful when deviating from it. Let me explain.

The team commander of our Afghan partner force in 2010 had been hovering around my vehicle for a few moments. I could tell he wanted to speak to me, and that he was waiting until the time was right—which meant until there was no one around except for me and the interpreter.

Our partner force was a militia. Matullah Khan, a powerful, millionaire warlord, commanded them. He was the type of man who rises up when law and order crumbles. His men weren't from the Afghan police or army, but they controlled the region. Khan was a pig of a man, if I'm honest, and was always very abrupt with me, arrogant even after my men had saved his in fight after fight.

In all, I worked with three partner force team commanders. The first guy was an old mujahedin fighter—he was like a grandfather to everyone, and tactically very proficient, but he couldn't keep up any longer in the field and so he was replaced. This current guy lacked any skill: he was a standover merchant, forever exploiting the locals. Rumour followed him—that he was a killer and that I had to watch him. His lack of humility amused me, and I found myself fascinated by some of his behaviour. His ego, while hard to manage, was also a great tool to exploit. In the months to follow, he was replaced by Abdul Nhabi, who was the complete opposite and a true Afghan patriot.

We hadn't been in the secure location long. We were out in the middle of the desert. I had my vehicles arranged in a tactical pattern. The primary weapons systems of each gun car pointed towards the mountains in the distance. Our mortars were set up and there was a commando with a pair of binoculars on every other vehicle, ordered to scan the horizon for anyone daft enough to mess with what I liked to call HMAS *Yankee*, the inland battleship.

The heat of the day was slowly giving way to another freezing night, and like everyone else I was looking forward to some fresh food and a can of soft drink after spending the last few days on foot, clearing target villages in our area of operations. We had been looking for weapons caches, bomb-making equipment and intelligence.

During the clearance operation we had come across a Taliban stronghold. The usual firefight had taken place, and surprisingly the enemy hadn't fled after the first skirmish. My initial thought was that they'd run out of options—that they had nowhere go. However, as we looked around the large plantation where the combat had taken place, I could see there were multiple escape routes; they could have disengaged and saved themselves.

Then Commando Team Three came across the reason they had stayed to fight and die. One of the rooms in the compound contained twenty or so resin opium bricks. The dirty brown and tar blocks were used to make the highest-quality heroin in the world.

We loaded the bricks into one of our Bushmasters and destroyed the enemy's weapons and drug-making equipment. The crops had largely been stripped already; I considered burning the leftovers but thought better of it. It would probably assist them in readying the land for the next season.

In Afghanistan in 2010, we hadn't yet started working with the US Drug Enforcement Administration (DEA), so the procedures for a circumstance like this hadn't been well worked out. I understood, though, that confiscating the Taliban drugs and destroying their equipment would hinder their finance efforts, and I weighed this against the impact on the surrounding villages. We very rarely learnt who owned the plantations; I suspected the true owners had been killed years before. I could only look at the situation through narrow optics; I was sure it was far more complicated than I could understand.

We had taken a few prisoners, too, during this mission; one of them was actually a heroin addict. This wasn't the first time I had seen this in Afghanistan. He shook uncontrollably and was sweating profusely. At first we suspected he was a suicide bomber, and perhaps, if given the chance, he would have been. Many suicide bombers in Afghanistan were Pakistani addicts or HIV carriers. Some too sick to walk very far, so they'd drive the vehicle-borne IEDs.

The Afghan partner force had given this man a kicking before my men intervened, not just because it was highly unprofessional, but also because we had an Army photographer attached to us for this mission, and an Afghan journalist. The last thing I wanted was for a photo to be taken of an Afghan security guy kicking a Pakistani junkie to death. We were trying to provide the Afghan population with an alternative to the Taliban's violent rule.

'I need to speak with you urgently,' the Afghan team commander said through my interpreter.

'Can it wait until we have secured the location?' I asked, not wanting to be drawn into a long argument with him, which was how they all ended up.

'No,' came the reply. 'It is vital.'

I looked around; my men were going about their afternoon business. Weapons were being cleaned and vehicles serviced, while the prisoners were being questioned. Some men were preparing a fire for a barbecue that we would have that evening. Being vehicle-mounted and beyond the range of enemy weapons allowed us to enjoy some much-needed respite, and a steak and can of Coke does wonders for a man's morale. I always tried to include something like this when I was the ground force commander. Honestly, it was the best job on earth.

I nodded to the 'terp' that we could have a chat, and he asked the Afghan what was wrong. Immediately the two of them became engrossed in a deep discussion. It became a little heated, as it often did. A few of the Afghan's men came over and added their two cents' worth to the discussion, until finally the terp turned back to me.

'He wants you to give him the opium bricks, so he can take them back to Tarin Kowt.'

My mind raced, considering what he had to gain from this. Immediately I thought about jurisdiction: who was in control of this stuff, the legal considerations, my headquarters and what they would want. I had already reported the find, so it wasn't like I could just rock up without it. I suddenly found myself in a really shitty situation.

'That's not going to happen,' I replied.

'He said he needs them, and that it's their job to make sure that this is all handled correctly. His boss has ordered him to take control of any drugs that are found. He says he has a legal responsibility.'

It seemed very strange that the Afghan commander was suddenly so concerned with being professional. I'd had issues with him over the past two months because he never did any of the work I asked of him. I'd involved him in planning, and I'd sought his help in organising training for his men, but he never came through. His men were a rabble. Their equipment didn't fit and they never brought along the right gear. I was meant to use them as the face for all our operations, but they weren't trained like the local commandos with whom the US Special Forces operated, and they weren't as keen as the police force.

When I look back on this time now, I see that there were many things I could have done differently to help him, but at the time I was struggling to get all my own work done. I had to train my platoon, prepare for missions, sort out my own equipment and be a leader for my men; I didn't have time to babysit the partner force commander.

'That's not happening,' I said again.

I moved to walk away, but the Afghan yelled for me to stop. My platoon sergeant heard this and started walking over, and a couple of other commandos followed him.

The Afghan said a few more things to the terp, who smiled and nodded his head.

'Boss, his cousin is to be married in a few weeks,' he told me. 'He wants to give him two of the resin blocks as a wedding present. It is an old custom in Afghanistan.'

I looked at Paul Cale, whose bullshit meter, just like mine, was off the chart. He didn't laugh, though; he simply raised his eyebrows and looked back at me. I could almost hear him saying, 'How you gunna handle this one, boss?'

That was when I laughed. An old tradition of Afghans giving each other drugs as wedding presents? I knew now that he was talking bullshit.

The Afghan commander asked for the bricks a few different ways, and the story changed each time. He then followed me around the perimeter while I checked my guys' positions. At times he pleaded with me, and at other times he outright threatened to report me to Matullah Khan. Finally, he told me that I wasn't helping Afghanistan. Unless I handed the bricks over for them to take back to their security headquarters, I was part of the problem. Apparently, I wasn't taking my role seriously.

'Does it mean that much to you?' I asked.

He replied that it meant everything.

By now I'd had enough, and I worked out a plan on the spot. I asked the terp to tell the team commander that I'd discuss it with him over dinner tonight, and we'd work out a solution. For now, could he get his men ready for the next day's patrol? He rushed off, like a kid after you tell them they can have that bike they've been pestering you for. For the first time in two months, he barked orders and got his men motivated and moving.

While the Afghan partner force were busy cleaning weapons and embracing their newfound professionalism, I briefed my team commanders, the platoon sergeant and intelligence operator. They smiled at my plan.

Late in the afternoon, we gathered around the fire, which had burnt down to a smouldering pile of coals. One of the commando teams was busy preparing the steaks. Being this far out in the desert, and surrounded by over twenty large vehicles, a stores truck, 6x6 long-range patrol vehicles and numerous radio masts, I wasn't too worried about being seen by the enemy. They knew we were here.

My intelligence corporal and platoon sergeant JJ came over to me and handed me some paperwork. I smiled at them both and signed it. 'All done, lads?' I asked.

'Almost, boss,' JJ said, giving me a heavy brown paper bag.

We walked over to the fire, and I called the rest of the platoon over. I gave them an update of the mission over the last three weeks, and asked them to stay focused for the final week. I talked about our partner force and how good they had been, and then I called them to come into the circle with me. As I thought he might, the photographer was busy taking photos.

I shook hands with the Afghan team commander and gave him and the camera a big smile, and he did the same. Then I made a speech about how he wanted to protect his home and his countrymen, and how we were working well together on all the issues. As I was talking, I opened the brown paper bag and took out two opium bricks, then handed him one. He looked a little confused, but I kept talking.

Holding up my brick, I spoke about how this opium represented Afghanistan's violent past, and how the team commander and I would show everyone here that we were looking forward to a better future. With that I threw my brick onto the fire, then I turned to the Afghan and nodded. The commandos and the Afghan's own men added words of encouragement; there were a few cheers and some laughter.

He looked at the brick for a moment, and then tossed it onto the coals. I heard the camera clicking as he did.

We watched the bricks burn, and black smoke billow into the sky. The poisonous substance disintegrated quickly, and in a few minutes there were only coals and embers once more.

'Let's eat,' I said.

And with that we cooked our steaks and cracked open some cold cans of Coke. I'm not entirely sure why, but that steak was one of the most memorable of my life. Perhaps it was because I'd been eating rations for so long, or maybe it was the cut of the meat, but it hit the spot perfectly. If you haven't had steak cooked over opium coals, you probably don't know what I'm talking about.

The Afghan came over to me later and asked about the rest of the bricks. I looked confused, and asked what he was talking about. We had destroyed them all, I told him. The last two were the ones we'd thrown onto the fire as a symbol of how the country was moving forward. I thanked him again for his help, then I walked off, leaving him there in silence. We never spoke of it again.

A few days later, the platoon returned to Tarin Kowt and I went and saw my company commander. I handed him the paperwork for the two bricks we had destroyed, and let him know that my platoon was currently handing over the remaining drugs to the company sergeant major, who would organise to have them handed over to the DEA. The Americans would test the drugs and ultimately destroy them.

A week later, an article appeared in the local newspaper in Tarin Kowt. The Afghan team commander was smiling in the first photo, and then throwing an opium brick into the fire in the second photo. He took off, fleeing Tarin Kowt, but I was told he didn't get far. I wasn't upset. He had proven to me that he didn't believe in a peaceful Afghanistan—in fact, his actions were those of a sympathiser. I had no doubt the drugs would have passed into the hands of the enemy, had I relinquished them.

Abdul Nhabi replaced him, and for the first time I had an Afghan team commander who was brave, professional and dedicated to the task. My job had suddenly become exponentially easier. Nhabi fought bravely on many occasions, and he pushed his men hard and demonstrated integrity. I'm proud to call him a brother in combat.

Nhabi fought on for many years after I left. During his adult life, he knew nothing but war. The Afghanistan conflict truly was a generational one, and I don't doubt that his sons, who would now be in their early twenties, are continuing the fight. Sadly, Nhabi himself was killed in a vehicle IED attack. RIP, Abdul. I hope your country can one day become the place you and I discussed, the place I know you desired it to be.

Abdul Nhabi was an honest man and we shared many a conversation about leadership and the future of his team. I told him how I had deliberately deceived the previous commander and we discussed the rumours that now surrounded his demise. The lesson, I said, was how dishonesty can also be a weapon—there can be unintended consequences for being deliberately deceptive or for accidentally lying.

LESSONS

An adult lifetime of working in leadership positions has taught me that honesty and integrity are vital principles to maintain.

Sometimes you will work with people who have a different set of standards to you, and think they can get away with doing the wrong thing. All you can do is maintain a high moral standard and seek to practise it constantly.

25

PROFESSIONALISM

'We're trying to get the SEAL community back to where we think it should be—quiet professionalism.'

William H. McRaven

It is ironic that I would choose the William McRaven quote as my chapter quote given that as an ex-Special Operations officer publishing a mentor-style leadership book I am not exactly going quietly. Nor is the irony lost on me that McRaven's first book *Spec Ops: Case studies in Special Operations warfare* was one of the most influential books of my career. I assume he wrote it while conducting quiet professionalism. But I am of the very firm belief that after a life of service we owe it to share lessons we've learnt so that others can draw on our experiences to help guide them on their own leadership journeys. One of McRaven's most recent book is *Make Your Bed: Little things that can change your life . . . and maybe the world* and as far as quiet professionalism goes, it's worth a read.

So what have I learnt about professionalism? The secret is to know your job and keep your emotions in check.

Back in 2007 I was the Officer in Charge of the Selection Wing, responsible for the mechanics of the SAS and Commando regiments' selection courses. One day I bumped into Lieutenant Colonel L by chance, while walking between meetings. After the pleasantries, I asked him about my chances of returning to the regular commando unit as a platoon commander the following year.

He looked at me in silence for a moment, considering my question. Then he calmly explained that all the positions were full; perhaps there was an operations officer job, but I shouldn't count on it.

I rolled my eyes, shook my head and snorted my displeasure.

'You don't have a very good poker face, do you, Bram?' he said in response.

The comment hurt me—not for the way it was said, but because of the person who had said it. Lieutenant Colonel L was considered one of the brightest officers in the Army, let alone the Special Forces. And it felt like he'd just insulted me.

We talked some more about other things, then went our separate ways. Through the remainder of that day, and for many years afterwards, I thought about his comment. What did it even mean to say I didn't have a good poker face?

My Commanding Officer, Lieutenant Colonel K, the commander of the Special Forces Training Centre, had assured me he was working hard to get me back to the unit as a platoon commander. I had been told what a great job I had done that year. My comment to Lieutenant Colonel L was no more than idle chitchat, but I had uncovered some of the politics that were playing out behind the scenes, which until now I hadn't been aware of. That had shocked me, and I hadn't been able to hide my surprise—and Lieutenant Colonel L had called that out. He'd straight-out criticised my emotional reaction!

Because of my background as an officer who'd come from within the ranks, I was looked at differently by many of the officers. I was what was known as a 'changeover', a senior non-commissioned officer who had attended a selection board and been deemed suitable to be granted a commission. Until I was commissioned, my peers were the other Special Forces sergeants and a few warrant officers, many of whom I had attended promotion courses with. I suppose I was considered a high performer, or at least above the average. I had been disappointed by the standard of some of my Regular Army peers on my promotion courses, and because of that I had tried all the harder to dominate the courses. In the process I'd ruffled a few feathers and made some enemies—some I didn't even know were enemies. They became apparent when I changed over.

The other non-commissioned officers ostracised me: as far as they were concerned, I was a traitor. Some of them back in the unit were happy to see the back of me. The reception from the officers was a little different, but they still treated me with scepticism and suspicion; after all, I wasn't a 'real' officer. I found myself, for the first time during my Army career, with no real friends.

By my third year as a captain, and as the Officer in Charge of Selection for Special Forces, I had decided that the best revenge was to be successful. I was going through a heartbreaking marriage break-up at the time, which I look back on now and take full ownership for. (Of course, at the time it would have been everybody's fault but mine.) I immersed myself in my life as the OIC of Selection.

I moved back onto base and into a room in the officer's mess. My daily schedule was that of a warrior. I got up at 4 am and ran, then unit physical training at 07.30, then it was work, swim at lunch and the gym after work. By night I would study modules for my degree. I did this all day every day, five days a week. Then I'd go to Sydney on the weekend and be drunk in Kings Cross the whole time. I was living a brutal and highly disciplined life. I demanded excellence from my staff and myself, and I didn't really care about how it was achieved.

So when Lieutenant Colonel L pointed out a weakness like that, it cut me to the bone.

Over the next few months, I watched many candidates go through the Special Forces pipeline. I saw traits in the men that I also saw in myself, some good and some bad, but after that conversation with Lieutenant Colonel L, one of the things I noticed the most was who had a bad poker face. There was something to this, more than I'd realised.

The fact was that people who showed their emotions were thought less stable than people who didn't. Some candidates would be 'binned' altogether because they couldn't control their emotions.

That was when I started to develop my understanding of professionalism, and what it means to be professional. There was more to it than knowledge, skills and attitude. These were the building blocks of professional mastery, for sure, but to be deemed a professional you needed something else—there was another layer.

Plenty of Special Forces candidates showed that they had professional mastery, but they weren't able to control their emotions. I once watched an officer from an infantry battalion lose his cool over the smallest issue. He had been deemed highly competent. He was a platoon commander from a reconnaissance platoon, and as such he had completed one of the most demanding mental and physical courses the infantry has to offer. Capable of navigating across country, carrying heavy loads and in arduous terrain, he had reinforced this during the Special Forces navigation exercise.

Then, on one cold winter morning of the selection course, the officer was tasked with resubmitting a plan to the Commanding Officer that he had failed the night before. He was drinking a cup of coffee at the time, and talking to some fellow candidates who were also waiting for further instruction. On receiving the news, he threw his coffee to the ground, replying, 'For fuck's sake!' That was enough for him to receive a 'pink slip', the form used to issue a formal warning to a candidate.

I watched this unfold in front of me. He stormed off to the barracks and grabbed his TEWT board. A TEWT is a Tactical Exercise Without Troops, and orders are presented with the aid of a large wooden board that contains maps and plastic overlays. TEWTs are a terrific way to test the mechanics of a plan without soldiers actually being deployed. As he left, I noticed the Commanding Officer watching from afar. He had witnessed the whole thing. This didn't bode well for the candidate.

The candidate presented his plan. As the OIC of Selection, I sat in on the presentation so that I could quality-control the session. The Commanding Officer would determine the pass or fail mark, based on the officer meeting certain criteria. The plan was well delivered and the mechanics were solid—it was a far better performance than he'd made the night before, and I could see that the Commanding Officer was impressed.

'Well done,' he said. 'Solid plan.'

'Thanks, sir,' the young officer replied, and he packed up his board and returned to the barracks to prepare for the next session.

'What do you think, Captain Connolly?' the CO asked.

'He's solid, boss. A good candidate.'

The CO thought about this, and looked at me for what seemed like an eternity. 'Nope, I disagree,' he said at last. 'He's unable to control himself emotionally, and wears his heart on his sleeve. I'll be surprised if he gets through the next week.'

I was shocked—for me he was the standout candidate, tall, powerfully built and smart. He seemed the epitome of the Special Forces officer. I had much to learn.

Within the week, that officer withdrew from the course. He was being ridden by the Training Wing staff. The Selection Wing staff were riding him too, writing him up daily for attitude; it seemed the guy couldn't get out of his own way. He lost his mind at the smallest setback, and talked to the other candidates within his group like they were useless. He was a poor leader.

When he left the selection course, I thought some more about professionalism. It was more than skills, knowledge and attitude, although perhaps his attitude was questionable. To the more experienced professional officers, there were additional traits that mattered: presence, personality and patience.

LESSONS

Professionalism means keeping your cool and making considered decisions when confronted with challenging situations.

Frank but fair opinions are valuable, but the way they are delivered can cause problems.

Your conduct and demeanour dictate the behaviour and responses of the people around you. If you're inappropriately emotional, this can have an adverse effect. Showing anger at a decision from your superiors, especially in front of subordinates, sets them and also you up for failure when you have to motivate them and implement the plan.

Make your bed in the morning—because McRaven says to, and also because doing the little things right is what makes a professional.

26

TOLERANCE

'We were all humans until race disconnected us, religion
separated us, politics divided us, and wealth classified us.'

attributed to Banksy

There are cultural differences across the world, shared norms and practices that look foreign to an outsider. I've encountered supposedly 'primitive' peoples who understand this concept acutely. If they can be tolerant of other, different cultures, surely Westerners can too. Take a moment to imagine a world where everyone was culturally the same—how boring that would be!

It was in Chora, Afghanistan, that I learnt how cultural tolerance can be a leadership superpower. I placed my Steiner binoculars on the hood of the Bushmaster. From the overwatch position, out on the open desert plateau, I could see that the structure we'd designated as 'the White Building' was heavily defended. The only thing separating us from it was a few kilometres of sand and rock, and the vegetation of the thick Green Belt. A flowing stream and a culvert choke point were the main obstacles we had to contend with.

I looked around at my platoon; all the men were going about their business. They were mostly in shorts, body armour and baseball caps, and were kicking up dust as they moved around our assembled vehicles, packing equipment, conducting final weapons and radio inspections, and organising the items required for this afternoon's meeting.

I had been tasked with talking to the governor of the area and his chief of police, with the meeting to be held at the White Building. My mission was fairly simple: keep them onside, don't promise more than we could deliver, and try to elicit a specific piece of information about a known Taliban sympathiser in the area, someone who was possibly within the police force.

This sympathiser had been sending information to the Taliban, and we had reason to believe he was also either digging in IEDs, or at the very least shipping the parts around the valley for someone. In recent months, the relationship between the Special Operations Task Group and the police in Chora had risen to a new high. We were helping them build capacity in the township, thanks mostly to the efforts of the previous rotation of commandos.

The White Building was secured on all corners by the police, and there were roadblocks leading from the desert all the way to the front gate. The Afghan National Army patrolled the Green Belt. It was clear this would be an important meeting for everyone concerned.

The previous day, we'd had a close call as we entered outer Chora. We had startled a militia roadblock manned by police officers in plain clothes. Our forward vehicle had rounded a corner and surprised them. My men were equally surprised. The only reason we didn't initiate was that we'd rolled onto them so fast. We'd had no indication they were in the area.

At first they looked to be about to flee, which would undoubtedly have ended with us taking up pursuit. But they controlled their reaction courageously. Once we'd checked their documents and radioed their headquarters, their identities were confirmed. Truth be told, I was surprised to learn they were legit.

After watching the White Building for a few more hours, I developed a plan. We would roll our whole armada straight into town—it would be a show of force. We would position our vehicles on the street behind the compound. Twelve Bushmasters made for a large signature, but it also meant business. Remote weapons stations, four teams of commandos, engineers, dogs and an Afghan response team—anyone attacking us would be doing so on the last day of their lives.

After we pulled up at the designated position, I made the short walk from my command vehicle to the White Building with a couple of commandos, my interpreter and my intelligence analyst. We all conceal-carried Heckler & Koch USPs, but left our body armour behind. The platoon's 'actions-on' that would cover our various plans dependent on the changing situation were extensive, and I was confident I had thought of every angle, should I need support or should something happen where the vehicles were parked.

I enjoyed this type of intellectual challenge. It was classic counter-insurgency. I had studied International Studies at university, with a major in societies, and I felt equipped and qualified to capably conduct these 'white space operations' (missions that support the reconstruction effort or a non-government agency effort). I had briefed the platoon that this would be 'CO-IN to contact': we would use counterinsurgency to locate ourselves in the best position, and then conduct ambushes or other sophisticated operations, leveraging off the information we had gained.

Arriving at the White Building, we were warmly welcomed and then ushered inside. We took sweet cardamom tea and exchanged small talk about the weather and crops. The governor and I discussed security and how we might help them further. I promised nothing but agreed to further meetings.

Then I asked the Afghans about their concerns and issues, many of which I had heard a million times before. They fought each other verbally to be the first to tell me they needed more money, more men, more vehicles, a new school, a new drinking well, the roads needed to be fixed and so on.

Soon, though, we were joined by another group and the mood changed. This was a smaller faction from the police, with members from different family and tribal lines, and the two groups were having trouble agreeing on anything. The room fell silent. I tried to spark up some more conversation, but no one was speaking. The meeting was going nowhere.

My primary objective, of course, was to find out a name for a known Taliban sympathiser within the police, and this would be a huge coup. Was he even here at this meeting?

The conversation wrapped up and I moved to leave, but the governor pressed us to stay for a late lunch. Almost at the same time, servers arrived with three huge platters of steaming goat stew and an endless supply of flatbread.

My mind immediately turned to hygiene: would it be safe to eat this food? Not once in all my days in Afghanistan had I suffered gastro. I put my good fortune down to drinking bottled water and washing my hands regularly—basically, to adhering to the principles of hygiene. I had only eaten the local food once, and this had been a matter of urgency. We'd been trapped in a valley for a few days without food, and had paid some locals richly to make us dinner— and then made them eat half of it in front of us to ensure it hadn't been poisoned. We ate well and were fine.

At the White Building, we sat cross-legged in a rectangle around long, colourful mats. Bowls were passed around and the Afghans used pieces of flatbread to scoop up the oily orange slop and pile it onto their plates. I judged that eating large pieces of meat would be best, and I knew to avoid the head, tongue and anything that looked like tripe.

As we began eating, the conversation became more expansive. My interpreter talked to me in hushed tones, explaining the political conversations taking place around us. I ate and tried to seem thoughtful, but I wasn't really paying much attention as the food was that good! I shovelled it in and then cleaned my plate with the flatbread.

The chief of police had cracked open the goat's skull, and the Afghans quarrelled for a time over who would eat the brain. A similar pantomime was conducted over the tongue and eyes, and soon the beast's head was a bare skull. Everyone was having seconds now, so I helped myself to what was left on the main platter: four big chunks of bone and meat and some orange gravy.

Now the conversation was going in earnest. The men seemed to have forgotten some of their family issues, and there was even a bit of good-natured laughter here and there. A question was posed directly to me, and my interpreter explained what was being asked.

I thought deeply about my response and provided a few words, then picked up a piece of meat from the plate with my hands and started to gnaw on it. I pulled the meat and gristle away from the bone with my teeth; it snapped back with a satisfying crack. The room fell silent, and I looked up.

The Afghans were all gazing at me, their mouths agape. Some shook their heads and looked away, apparently in disgust; others narrowed their eyes in criticism. Two or three had furrowed brows and were biting their lips.

The governor said something, which was repeated around the room. The men were all shaking their heads and then nodding in agreement. They flung down their bowls, discarded them on the tapestry, and shot glances left and right. Twenty-odd people were staring at me in anger.

I tuned to my interpreter. 'What the hell is going on?'

He chuckled under his breath and looked down at his feet. 'They called you a fucking savage, boss,' he whispered.

I was seriously confused. I had just witnessed these men tearing the remains of this beast apart, including its head and internal organs—and I was the savage? I looked all the Afghans in the eyes.

'Boss?' One of my commandos was trying to make sense of the situation. I could sense his confusion as the tension in the room mounted.

I turned back to my interpreter. 'I don't understand. Please ask them why they're calling me that.'

I became aware of my USP in the paddle holster against my body, and noted the AK-47s leaning against the wall behind the Afghans. The bullet holes I spotted along the wall further heightened my situational awareness. I could sense the two commandos behind me slowly moving apart, so as to gain a better angle should they need to draw their weapons. My heart rate increased slightly as the adrenaline kicked in.

The interpreter asked some more questions in Pashtu, and responses were spat around the room with venom. The interpreter sniggered, as did the police chief, who was picking his nose at the time—I remember that very clearly.

'Boss,' said the interpreter, 'he said that anyone who eats the feet of a goat is a savage. You have no morals and haven't been brought up very well.'

The look on my face as I was told this must have been priceless. Instantly the Afghans began rolling around like six-year-old kids, feet in the air, holding their bellies. Some wiped tears of laughter away, and others hugged the friend next to them. A few jumped up and came over to me, placing their heads on my shoulders and patting me on the back as they cried with laughter. One guy picked up some meat and mimicked me eating, and they laughed all the harder.

I laughed too—nervously at first, and then raucously.

After a while everyone settled down and we got back to our conversation. The Afghans now spoke freely and with passion about their community, and the positive steps being taken towards a bright future. More tea was offered and consumed. All in all, it was a great afternoon.

Just before nightfall and our departure, when I sensed the time was right, I politely asked the assembled group for silence, and then I asked a question of my own. A Taliban sympathiser's fate was sealed, seemingly by the foot of a goat.

LESSONS

Encountering different cultures can be difficult, and even dangerous. But if you show a willingness to engage, and demonstrate humility and good humour, you will likely be successful.

Immerse yourself into new environments with an open mind. Try to look beyond superficial differences, and treat those around you as equals.

27

HUMILITY

'You can't get fat eating humble pie. I eat lashings
of it and it's never affected my weight.'

So, you can't get fat eating humble pie. What exactly do I mean by that?

As a leader I found humility to be a powerful resource when it came to motivating subordinates. It was actually on my first deployment as an operations officer of a commando company when I realised that the soldiers under my command responded better when I stood in front of them and said I had made a mistake or that they were right and let's go with their plan. I also learnt at around the same time not to have an emotional attachment to a strategy or to a way of doing things because the chances were that there would be other opinions out there and ultimately we would come up with better plans. So not being emotionally attached in the first instance also helps with being humble.

Humility can be a great tool to help people collaborate, allowing them to bring their experiences together to solve a problem. I don't like using the term 'safe environment', but I do think there has to be a level of safety when it comes to sharing opinions and experiences, and only the humble leader can create this high mark.

The idea is that it's not bad for you to show some humility. I learnt this later in my career, around the time I was working for Tim Curtis, an officer who came to the Commando Regiment from SASR to raise its counter terrorist capability. One of the things he used to say was 'be humble in defeat and gracious in victory'. The other was that 'life is a daily renewable contract'. Both these sayings speak of a type of inner strength, perhaps even stoicism.

Let me explain a little about what humility actually is . . . It's about how you view your own importance in the grand scheme of things. It's how you respond to being right, as well as how you respond to being wrong. How people respond to being wrong gives me a good indication of the type of person I'm dealing with. If they throw their toys out of the pram, suffice to say they probably have a higher regard for themselves than the situation itself. I do judge people on how they respond to not wining or to not being right.

So, let me explain for a moment what humility is not . . . it isn't self-deprecation or being submissive. In fact, on those days when I am eating lashings of humble pie, I find that it is actually a position of power. Acknowledging that I was wrong about something can catch people off guard.

Being humble is a great way to learn to be authentic and self-aware. Having humility means that you know you make mistakes. If you can remove your armour and forgive yourself then you can forgive others for making a mistake as well. When people know this, they will be braver about experimenting and searching for better solutions. As a leader this is a great outcome.

––––––

Going hand-in-hand with the tools we carry is the armour we wear. When I think about it, I saw this continuously throughout my career, but I never really understood it. Much of my career in the Army was built on the idea of 'fake it til you make it'. But hiding behind a false persona will eventually bring a person unstuck. It's better to know who you truly are, stripped of your armour, than it is to project an image that you can't back up when it counts.

We all wear armour—it's a natural self-protective mechanism. What other people think of us matters to us, and that's shaped by the words we use, the clothes we wear and the opinions we hold. Yet some of my most memorable moments have come when I've put down my armour and ventured out, naked, with no protection from the thoughts or comments of others.

After I left the Army in 2011 I went to work for a consultancy firm. I was engaged by a large industrial company to review their emergency action plan, and provide a quote for any gaps that might exist or amendments that might be needed. This work required me to have fortnightly meetings with the company's management.

About three months in, I was presenting to the senior staff about some shortfalls in their current crisis-management plan. These went against what the firm believed to be best practice.

When I was done, one of our client's senior executives leant back in his seat and commented that we just wanted their money. 'There's nothing wrong with our existing plan,' he stated. Then he added, 'What would you really know about this shit anyway?'

I remember my feelings at the time. I was enraged—not because he was a fat, red-faced, opinionated old fool, but because tension had been building up between us for a while. I hadn't been able to get him onside, or at the very least nullify his continual attacks on our consultancy. I was trained to win battles, not wars.

The specific gap that I'd identified concerned the company's next-of-kin notification plan. It had the CEO, who was also the owner of the company, personally delivering all notifications to the direct relatives of deceased workers. I argued that this wasn't best practice for the business due to the location of the CEO; it would be much better if certain senior management at each state site were trained to act on behalf of the company. Moreover, if there were multiple fatalities in different states, the CEO couldn't possibly fulfil his duties under the plan. This meant families would most likely learn about their deceased loved one from the breaking news.

After the executive questioned my knowledge, I slowly stood from my chair, figuratively putting on my body armour. I was no longer the hired crisis-management consultant who had been forced to operate within a corporate framework; I was Major Bram Connolly, DSM, of the Special Forces. I stood tall, my chest out and my eyes narrowed. I was looking forward to this.

People who know me will tell you I have a look when I've been pushed to *that* point. I was already engaged with this man in combat; truth be told, I'd probably subconsciously set these events in motion as a type of ambush for him. I wasn't in control of what Major Connolly said or did next; in fact, I rather wanted to let him do his thing.

'I'll tell you what I know,' I began forcefully. 'My background is in the Special Forces. I've had to do mandatory notification planning before. I've seen callout teams deployed across multiple states after critical incidents, tasked with telling the parents and partners of some of the finest men this country has ever raised and deployed the heartbreaking news that their sons and husbands were dead. Unlike in your industry, we give a fuck about telling them with respect and dignity.'

The room fell silent.

My own boss, an ex-artillery lieutenant colonel, was there too. His jaw was almost on the table. I had thrown up my shield for protection, grabbed my sword and slashed this idiot executive from ear to bowel. I stood there in the silence, feeling like a glorious warrior as the colour washed from my enemy's fat face. I glared down at him.

Then I looked around the room and my body armour dissolved. I felt like a complete idiot. Instantly I grasped that I'd failed to navigate this problem without making it personal. Rather than educate this executive respectfully, I had attacked him at his most vulnerable moment. The moment he'd shown his ineptness, I had shoved the solution down his throat. As I said, I was trained to win battles, not wars.

I sat down and my boss took over. Skilfully, he took the senior staff on a journey, explaining the current problems and their implications, and then presenting a raft of possible solutions. I sat there fuming, my hands sweaty and my pulse racing—not because of the fat nobody, who was still reeling from the interaction, but because of my reaction to him. I was furious with myself.

In the taxi on the way back to the office, my boss made it clear what he thought of my outburst. I knew I needed to do some serious soul-searching, and reflect on the way I engaged with others. Our relationship suffered as a result of my outburst; he didn't know if he could trust me. I didn't know how not to be emotive towards people for whom I didn't hold much respect. I've always struggled with that.

Some of my issues came from carrying around my armour. We all do it. If you're a businessperson, perhaps you wear a suit and tie and bark orders at your minions, or you wear high heels and expensive clothes that project your status. These are versions of armour: they protect you from the opinions of others, and shield you from your own self-doubt. My armour was my status and posture as a military leader.

I was reminded of an experience I had in Afghanistan a few years earlier. One warm summer night, with the moon almost full, my platoon and I were walking to a target. The way the moonlight cast our shadows against the clay walls of the target village made me feel slightly vulnerable.

Then I noticed my own shadow. My body armour made me look heavier, more muscular; the antenna projecting from my pack was like a beacon of professionalism. I had my night-vision goggles flipped up on my helmet, and they created a strange visual on the wall. All the equipment I was carrying, including my weapon, made my image look more professional than I felt. My shadow looked like a superior version of me.

Years later, when I was walking the dog early on a dark and wet morning in Perth, I saw my shadow from the street lights. That night in Afghanistan came flooding back to me, and I felt myself stiffen with pride. My self-image was bolstered by my memories of the warrior that I had been, and who I could become again, if needed. My identity as a Special Forces soldier had always been my shield.

Then I started thinking how I needed my shield to encompass more than this. I needed to be more rounded, smarter and better able to operate within civilian society. Moreover, I needed to be someone genuine—and I needed to understand who I was when my Special Forces identity had been stripped away. In short, I needed multiple shields, and I also needed to be comfortable taking off my shield and just being me.

Sometimes in meetings these days, I laugh to myself as I imagine a time when people don't wear clothes. If we were all gathered around this table naked, would these people be so confident to call each other out the way they do? The dynamic would be so different. Our physiques say a lot about our decisions and our willpower, and in some ways also our strength of character. We can cover up our short-falls or our penchant for excess with the clothes we wear.

If I'd been able to look at things from that perspective on that day in our client's office, perhaps I would have taken a less combative approach. I might have felt sorry for him, instead of deploying an attack that he had no ability to defend. Perhaps that's a secret of leadership during change management: just like in close combat, you should use only enough ammunition to achieve your task. I dropped a nuclear weapon on that guy when I could have achieved the same outcome using a silenced 9-millimetre pistol.

Today, I can see how I got myself to the point where that occurred. In the military we wear uniforms, and we become part of a team. In my case it was a high-performing and well-motivated team, and the strength of the wolf is its pack. My identity became nested in being part of that team.

But carrying that persona into the 'real world' was fraught with danger. My team wasn't there to support me. My uniform and rank weren't there either. With that executive, I was as forthright as I would have been with a young soldier, but I didn't have the *Defence Force Discipline Act* to support me. He was a civilian, and an important one in the context of that meeting. I had won the battle, but I wouldn't be around long enough to win that war.

I left my role with the consulting company a few months later, and went to the Middle East to be a cultural adviser to the Emiratis. I departed with a few life lessons. I remained on good terms with those I worked with, but I knew I needed some positive change. In the years that followed, I improved my ability to play the longer game.

This was a lesson I needed after leaving the Army. It's one I'm still learning.

LESSONS

We all have a tendency to put on our armour when we feel we have to defend ourselves. This is human nature, but that doesn't mean it's appropriate or sensible.

Engage others with humility by removing your armour. Take others with you, persevere when you're not succeeding, be gracious in defeat and yield ground when required. Be magnanimous in victory; remember, if your client or partner wins, then you win too.

CONCLUSION

One thing I've learnt through the process of writing this book is how solid my views are in some areas and how open to change I am in others. You'll probably agree that this isn't a bad problem to have.

I am still on my own path of self-development. In sharing with you some of my journey, as well as a lot of the mistakes I've made and the lessons I've learnt along the way, I hope I've opened you to the possibilities of self-reflection. By developing a deeper level of under-standing of yourself you will become a better person and ultimately a better leader. In fact, I would go so far as to say that the secret of life is as simple as pursuing personal self-development.

I haven't included everything I wanted to, in part because of national secrecy acts and in part because of my own failings as a person. Both are sufficiently potent as to make me think twice about what to put on the page in indelible ink.

This book is about resilience, optimisation, leadership and values, all areas worthy of our examination. I believe they are the pillars of self-development and as such require a degree of daily focus. I explore these four areas in detail with experts through my podcast *WarriorU*.

When I look back on my career, the highlight was 2010. I was a Special Forces Commando platoon commander leading five teams of specially selected and specially trained operators, all of them highly skilled. Every other experience I'd had in the Australian Defence Force was the platform for that role. And so it is for the challenges we have in our everyday lives. Everything that has tested you in the past is the foundation for how you will react or cope in the future. I hope that this book motivates you to develop yourself, to be ready for when your next unexpected test arrives.